D0584948

Financial Reporting by Private Companies: Analysis and Diagnosis

Principal Researcher:
A. Rashad Abdel-khalik
Coauthors:
William A. Collins
P. David Shields
Douglas H. Snowball
Ray G. Stephens
John H. Wragge

Financial Accounting Standards Board
of the Financial Accounting Foundation
HIGH RIDGE PARK, P.O. BOX 3821, STAMFORD, CONNECTICUT 06905-0821

657.95
A 13 f

FOREWORD

The FASB is considering financial reporting by private and small public companies. This consideration is in response to concerns about the relevance and costliness of certain information for those companies in applying generally accepted accounting principles. The FASB initially concluded that more information was needed about the specifics of those concerns to reconcile differing views and to focus on potential solutions to perceived problems.

As part of its efforts, the FASB commissioned this study on financial reporting by private companies, which was financed by the FASB, the National Association of Accountants, and the University of Florida. The principal researcher, Professor A. Rashad Abdel-khalik, and his colleagues have brought considerable research expertise to the issues and have devoted many hours to the detailed interviews and surveys that are part of the study.

This comparative analysis of practices and views of managers, bankers, and public accountants involved with private companies provides insights about the small business environment that need to be understood to assess existing financial reporting and the need for change. For example, the findings point out that some practices and perceptions of managers, bankers, and public accountants, as well as certain accounting pronouncements, contribute to the perceived problems regarding financial reporting by private companies.

This research report will provide useful information to the FASB and others in considering financial reporting issues concerning small business. We are grateful to the researchers, to those who provided financial support, and to the participants who willingly gave their time and shared their experiences and views regarding this important subject.

Stamford, Connecticut
August 1983

James J. Leisenring
Director of Research
and Technical Activities

i

PREFACE

This project was the product of a series of cooperative efforts. The participants, who kindly responded to our requests for interviews and completed the questionnaires, contributed the most. Due to their cooperation and candid expression of opinion we were able to come to grips with some complicated relationships. The role of the Advisory Committee was significantly helpful in developing the questionnaires. Members of the committee included: Allen D. Boyle (Dunmore Corporation), Jules M. Cassel (FASB), Thomas R. Dyckman (Cornell University), Glendon R. Hildebrand (FASB), Robert A. Klein (Midlantic National Bank), and Rholan E. Larson (Larson, Allen, Weishair & Co.). Many research assistants have participated in coding the data and in computing. In particular, I would like to express my appreciation to Ring D. Chen, Dimitrios Ghicas, Linda McDaniel, and Ramasamy Odaiyappa, who are all students at the University of Florida.

This project began when I was with the University of Florida and ended when I joined the faculty of the University of Illinois. The University of Florida's Accounting Research Center and the National Association of Accountants provided added financial support to augment the grant given by the FASB. In addition, Alfred M. King (NAA) provided helpful comments and arranged for NAA members to complete questionnaires. Much of the computing assistance and the typing of various drafts of questionnaires and hundreds of letters were provided by the Accounting Research Center. The University of Alberta, where I was a visiting professor in 1982-1983, provided typing assistance for three drafts of the final manuscript. The gracious assistance of Susan Stewart (University of Florida) and Joan Brown (University of Alberta) is very much appreciated.

Finally, I would like to express my appreciation to the FASB staff and particularly to Glendon Hildebrand, Patricia Kelly, Florence Mazzella, and Barbara Stout for their counsel and assistance throughout the work on this project.

Champaign, Illinois   A. Rashad Abdel-khalik
August 1983   Principal Researcher

iii

RESEARCH TEAM

Principal Researcher:

A. Rashad Abdel-khalik
Weldon Powell Professor of Accountancy and Director of Office of Accounting Research, University of Illinois at Urbana-Champaign

Coauthors:

William A. Collins
Associate Professor of Accounting, University of Florida

P. David Shields
Visiting Assistant Professor, University of Michigan and Assistant Professor, University of Florida

Douglas A. Snowball
Associate Professor of Accounting, University of Florida

Ray G. Stephens
Assistant Professor of Accounting, Ohio State University

John H. Wragge
Assistant Professor of Accounting, University of Delaware

RESEARCH REPORT

Financial Reporting by Private Companies:
Analysis and Diagnosis

CONTENTS

Page

CHAPTER 1—A SYNOPSIS

General Summary and Conclusions[1]

Financial statements should be helpful to the intended users in making decisions. Choices about accounting standards should be based on the information needs of those users. In addition, the constraint that the benefits of information must exceed the costs of providing and using it has to be considered. Accordingly, this research focuses on those information needs and on the costs and benefits of using generally accepted accounting principles (GAAP) for financial reporting by private companies.

Private companies prepare financial statements that are used primarily by managers and bankers. Accountants frequently participate in the preparation of those financial statements, but the direct cost of financial reporting is borne by the companies. However, the results obtained from interviews and surveys indicated that accountants generally are more concerned with the cost of financial reporting than are managers. Nonetheless, both groups perceive that the main cause of increased fees of accountants is inflation. Proliferation of accounting standards was perceived to have caused only about 20 percent of the increase.

The evidence also indicates that departures from GAAP occur moderately frequently for certain accounting standards, particularly for small companies. The cost of compliance and perceived lack of relevance to owners were rated as the primary reasons for those departures. In addition, certain accounting standards are perceived as overly complex, accounting for leases, deferred income taxes, and pensions being at the top of the list. Because of the difficulties with certain accounting standards, accountants and the nonrandom sample of managers believe that a special set of GAAP would be beneficial at least for private companies considered to be small in size. Managers of the random sample and bankers did not share that view.

GAAP financial statements for private companies are perceived to benefit both managers and bankers. Managers find GAAP financial

---

[1]The basis for these conclusions is presented at two levels in the report. The remainder of Chapter 1 is a detailed summary of the findings; Chapters 2-5 fully explain the methodology, analyses, and detailed results.

statements to be useful in making decisions and in facilitating borrowing. Bankers find that GAAP financial statements provide reliable and understandable data that are helpful in making lending decisions.

Furthermore, bankers have been accustomed to relying on accountants as the experts who provide the standards and verify adherence to them. Thus, bankers expressed concern about deviations from GAAP. They seem to feel that widespread deviations would dilute the credibility of the "expert" judgments they rely on. Nevertheless, bankers reported encountering deviations from GAAP. Although dealing with those deviations is situation-specific, in general, bankers revealed more tolerance of departures from GAAP than would have been deduced from their almost exclusive preference for GAAP.

Given their reliance on accountants as experts regarding financial information, bankers tend to associate GAAP financial statements of private companies with outside accountants. That is, they do not distinguish between the role of GAAP and the role of verification or review by outside accountants in providing useful financial statements. Thus, bankers tend not to distinguish questions regarding accounting standards setting from those involving the application of accounting standards. Consequently, their responses often reflected a mingling of the two functions.

The research findings indicate that bankers, managers, and accountants perceive cost-benefit considerations differently. That difference in perception brings questions about financial reporting by private companies into the political sphere, which is common when conflict of interest, not theory or rationality, dominates the issues. Research cannot resolve political problems; those problems have to be resolved by the joint working and directives of interested organizations.

As the researchers see it, the problem of cost-benefit considerations for reporting by private companies lacks clear identification with one authoritative body: Is it a practice problem (the domain of the American Institute of Certified Public Accountants (AICPA)), or is it a standards setting problem (the domain of the Financial Accounting Standards Board (FASB))? Based on the interviews, questionnaires, and review of the available literature and committee reports, the researchers conclude that the problem has elements of both practice and standards setting. Both organizations, the AICPA and the FASB, share the responsibility of maintaining the credibility of financial statements, including providing a satisfactory resolution to the problem at hand.

Introduction

Private companies are different from public companies in that their securities are not publicly traded. This difference has given rise to the issue of whether there should be different accounting standards for the two types of companies. Over the years, several committees of the AICPA have considered that issue.

Because the AICPA committees had identified certain problems that they felt resulted from existing accounting standards, the AICPA referred the matter to the FASB. In 1978, the FASB suspended the requirements for disclosure of earnings per share and segments for private companies, but the AICPA expected the FASB to do more to alleviate private companies of the burden of accounting requirements considered to be unnecessary and complicated.

In trying to assess concerns about financial reporting by private and small public companies, the FASB concluded that (a) there was no public consensus regarding the specifics of the perceived problems or their possible solutions and (b) more information was needed about the specifics in order to focus on developing possible solutions. For instance, the efforts by AICPA committees involved public accountants, but not managers and financial statement users of those companies. In addition, the public accountants had expressed diverse views on the issues. Also, the limited research by academicians regarding those companies had not provided conclusive results.

Accordingly, in 1981, the FASB undertook a major effort to obtain additional information about the practices and perceptions of managers, bankers, accountants, and others involved with financial reporting by private companies. As part of that effort, the FASB commissioned this research study.

Meanwhile, the AICPA has continued its consideration of the issues. In 1983, its Special Committee on Accounting Standards Overload has issued a final report in which the FASB is urged to reconsider and simplify certain accounting standards that are widely perceived to be unnecessarily burdensome and costly, especially for small, private companies.

Research Approach

This study focuses on three principal groups involved with financial reporting by private companies—management of those companies (managers), lending officers of commercial banks (bankers), and public accountants (accountants or practitioners). Each group has a different vantage point that must be considered in obtaining and interpreting feedback about the issues.[2]

The research approach adopted for each of the three groups involved several sequential steps in obtaining and analyzing information. After reviewing the authoritative literature on the subject, the researchers conducted exploratory interviews with a few managers, bankers, and accountants. The purpose of that initial step was to identify and delineate the essential issues that the research design should deal with.

The exploratory step was followed by extensive individual interviews with 29 bankers, 18 managers, and 31 accountants in 8 states. Those interviews were used to obtain additional information regarding issues generated from the exploratory interviews and to embellish the research design.

The interviews were followed by survey questionnaires, one for each of the three groups. The questionnaires addressed similar issues, but the questions were tailored to the special characteristics of each group.

---

[2]*Managers* of private companies need financial information to plan and control operations and typically provide financial statements to bankers and possibly others to obtain funds and enter into various activities. Some managers understand the specifics of GAAP, but many others do not. Many managers of small companies rely on outside accountants to prepare and interpret financial information.

Bankers, in supplying funds to private companies, need adequate information to make sound lending decisions. They use financial statements but do not have to purchase the financial information. Bankers typically are not experts on the specifics of accounting standards but need to understand the information produced by applying those standards.

Accountants assist private companies in preparing and interpreting financial statements and other financial information and also provide additional services to those companies. For many private companies, outside accountants apply complex accounting requirements and explain the requirements and results to company personnel. Accountants thus have a thorough knowledge of the intricacies of understanding and applying various accounting requirements, and their observations regarding experiences with companies, bankers, and others should be helpful.

The samples of participants in the questionnaire survey are presented below.

Sample	Nature of Sample Selection	Number Mailed	Number of Valid Responses
Managers	Random	530	99
Managers	Volunteered through chapters of National Association of Accountants (NAA)	112	72
Bankers	Members of The Robert Morris Associates—one in each member bank	554	129
Accountants	Primarily randomly selected from members of CPA societies in 12 states, excluding members of Big Eight firms	1,100	330
Accountants	From Big Eight firms (not random)	64	37

Some of the questions included in the questionnaires requested information about the respondents and their organizations. Certain characteristics of those organizations for each of the three groups are summarized on page 6 (more detailed profiles are in Chapter 4).

The final step in the research approach consisted of follow-up interviews by telephone with selected bankers and practitioners. Those interviews were intended to clarify and elaborate on the responses to the questionnaires.

Banks

Total assets		% of Responses
	Less than $ 50 million	13
	Less than $100 million	34
	Less than $200 million	60
	Less than $400 million	72

CPA Firms

		% of Responses
Number of	5 or fewer	71
partners	10 or fewer	86
per firm	40 or fewer	90

Private Companies

		% of Responses	
		Random Sample	NAA Sample
Total assets	$ 2 million or less	25	20
	$ 4 million or less	44	37
	$10 million or less	64	68
	$40 million or less	85	85

Questions Addressed

Answers were sought to the following basic questions:

1. Who are the users of financial statements of private companies?
2. How satisfactory is the information required by GAAP when applied to private companies?
3. How costly is the information required by GAAP when applied to private companies?
4. Have the difficulties in applying GAAP generated variations of or departures from GAAP?
5. How different are private companies from public companies relative to financial reporting?
6. What measures of size should govern if private companies were to be classified as small or large?
7. Do different sized private companies adopt different variations of GAAP?

8. How are different alternatives to GAAP perceived?
9. How do the responses from the Big Eight accounting firms compare with others?

A summary of the findings concerning each of these questions follows.

Who are the users of financial statements of private companies?

Responses by practitioners and managers to the questionnaires and in the interviews indicate that company managing owners are the primary users of financial statements of private companies, followed by bankers and suppliers.

How satisfactory is the information required by GAAP when applied to private companies?

Information was obtained about the degree of satisfaction with GAAP financial statements of private companies. Respondents were asked to evaluate the following characteristics that might be associated with such financial statements as compared with financial statements prepared on other bases, such as the cash basis:

1. Data quality: with respect to relevance, reliability, and understandability
2. Economic consequences on financing decisions: with respect to ease of financing, cost of financing, and extent of restrictive covenants
3. The relationship between the benefits of using GAAP and the fees of CPAs.

A majority of bankers and accountants expressed agreement with the statement that GAAP financial statements provide more reliable and relevant information for use by both managers and bankers. The managers were somewhat divided on this issue. A majority of all of the groups agreed with the statement that GAAP financial statements provide more understandable data.

Regarding economic consequences, all groups agreed that financing through debt is easier if private companies use GAAP, rather than another basis, for financial reporting. However, practitioners disagreed that GAAP results in lower borrowing costs and less restrictive covenants; bankers and managers were split in their opinions.

Finally, of those who expressed an opinion, about 90 percent of the bankers and about 60 percent of the managers from the random sample agreed that, on average, the expected benefits from using GAAP exceed the cost. Those managers in the NAA sample and the accountants were split regarding that relationship.

Responses to the question concerning the satisfaction with GAAP revealed that (a) bankers are the most satisfied with GAAP (as measured by the three dimensions of characteristics indicated above), (b) accountants and managers responding from the randomly selected sample have essentially the same degree of satisfaction with GAAP, but their views are less favorable than those of the bankers, and (c) the managers responding from the NAA sample are the least satisfied with GAAP.

A further validation of those perceptions was obtained by asking bankers and accountants to rate various reasons why bankers prefer GAAP financial statements over financial statements prepared on another basis. Bankers reasserted their belief that GAAP financial statements provide more relevant information, enable comparability among companies, and enable a better evaluation of debt-paying ability. Although accountants shared those views in general, about one-third of them disagreed with those propositions.

The evaluation of the benefits of GAAP also dealt with the extent to which accountants and managers face difficulties with specific accounting requirements. The accounting requirements considered were capitalization of leases, capitalization of interest on construction, accounting for deferred income taxes, accounting for pensions, accounting for compensated absences, preparing the statement of changes in financial position, accounting for contingencies, accounting for inventories at lower of cost or market, and discounting long-term receivables and payables.

Accountants and managers were asked to evaluate each of those accounting requirements on three qualitative dimensions: (a) complexity, (b) relevance to decision making by managers, and (c) relevance to outside users such as bankers. The results showed that three accounting requirements were considered to be highly relevant and not overly complex: preparation of the statement of changes in financial position, accounting for inventories at lower of cost or market, and accounting for contingencies. Accounting for compensated absences and capitalization of interest on construction were considered to be of less relevance to decisions, although they were not perceived to be overly complex. On the other hand, capitalization of leases and pension accounting were considered to be overly complex but of some relevance, especially to outside decision makers. Finally, accounting for deferred income taxes and discounting receivables and payables were considered to be relatively complex but not relevant.

Below is a summary of the relationship between relevance and complexity for those accounting requirements as perceived by the accountants and managers. Managers evaluated only those accounting requirements that were applicable to their own companies.

Degree of Relevance	Overly Complex	Not Overly Complex
Perceived as Relatively More Relevant to Decisions	(1) Capitalization of leases (2) Accounting for pensions	(1) Statement of changes in financial position (2) Accounting for inventories (3) Accounting for contingencies
Perceived as Relatively Less Relevant to Decisions	(1) Deferred income taxes (2) Discounting long-term receivables and payables	(1) Capitalization of interest on construction (2) Accounting for compensated absences

How costly is the information required by GAAP when applied to private companies?

The researchers attempted to evaluate whether the perceived causes of dissatisfaction with GAAP for private companies are in some way attributable to the increase in the cost of services of external accountants. Accountants and managers were asked to provide their views as to the causes of increases in accountants' fees during the past two years. One of the causes they were given to rate was the increased number and complexity of accounting standards; all other causes were external to standard setting. They included general inflationary conditions, changes in volume and size of business transactions, and improvements in internal reporting. The responses of the three groups—practitioners, managers of the randomly selected sample, and managers of the NAA sample—were strikingly similar. General inflationary conditions were rated as the primary cause to which about 40 percent of the fee increases was attributed. Rated next in importance was the increase in complexity and number of accounting standards, which was perceived to have caused about 20 percent of the fee increase. The other business-related reasons were considered responsible for most of the remaining increase in the fees charged by accountants. The increased number and complexity of accounting standards thus was perceived to have been responsible for a significant proportion of the increases in the accountants' fees, but was not considered to be the principal cause.

Managers also were asked to evaluate the benefits to their companies from using accountants' services versus the accountants' fees. Both samples of managers were divided between two opinions; that is, the fees charged in relationship to the expected benefits were about right or a little too high. Less than five percent of the respondents indicated that the fees were much too high in relationship to the benefits received.

In addition, managers were asked to identify the percentage of increase in fees that would make them dissatisfied with their accounting firm. Though the responses varied, the average response was 24 percent. Those responses validated the previous finding; namely, managers perceive that, on average, the benefits of preparing GAAP financial statements and engaging the services of accountants exceed the cost.

Information was sought about accountants' costs of keeping current with GAAP. Accountants were asked to indicate the annual number of hours that a practicing CPA in a firm like theirs must spend in studying accounting standards in order to remain current with GAAP. Accountants also were asked to specify the estimated number of hours each spends annually in keeping current with GAAP. Respondents indicated that an average of 91 hours per year ought to be spent to keep current, but only an estimated average of 54 hours per year is being spent.

Have the difficulties in applying GAAP generated variations of or departures from GAAP?

Accountants were asked to indicate the extent to which their private-company clients elect to depart from GAAP for each of the nine accounting requirements listed on pages 6 and 7, plus accounting for investments in related companies, in situations where the amounts are material. They also were asked to rate the following three reasons that may underlie departures from GAAP: relevance to decision making, cost, and consistency with the accounting basis used. The accountants provided separate ratings for small and large companies (based on their own perception of what constitutes small and large).

The least frequent departures from GAAP were reported for inventory valuation at the lower of cost or market, preparing the statement of changes in financial position, and accounting for contingencies. (As noted previously, accountants rated those three accounting requirements as relevant and not complex.) The most frequent departures from GAAP were reported for accounting for compensated absences and discounting long-term receivables and payables, for which about half of the respondents indicated departures all the time for small private companies. (As noted previously, accountants considered those accounting requirements to be not relevant to either managers or outside users.) In general, the reported frequency of departures from GAAP was significantly higher for small companies than for large companies.

The dominant reason for departing from GAAP for most of the accounting requirements was that alternatives were thought to be more relevant to decision making by owners. However, for accounting for pensions, compensated absences, and the statement of changes in financial position, the dominant reason for departure was the costliness of applying the requirements.

Bankers were asked to consider four accounting requirements with regard to departures from GAAP: accounting for deferred income taxes, the statement of changes in financial position, capitalization of interest on construction, and capitalization of leases. For each, bankers were asked to indicate the frequency with which they encounter deviations from or omissions of GAAP, the types of additional information they request in those situations, the frequency with which they receive the requested information, and the actions they take if the requested information is not provided.

Bankers indicated that the frequency of encountering known departures from GAAP is not high. Departures for capitalization of leases, capitalization of interest on construction, and accounting for deferred income taxes were reported to occur less frequently than for preparing the statement of changes in financial position. That statement was reported to be frequently omitted from the financial statements provided by borrowers, even though managers and accountants had indicated in their responses that the statement is relevant and that preparing it is not overly complex. The reaction of bankers to the omission of the statement of changes in financial position was either to develop it internally or to take no action. Most of the bankers indicated that the omission of the statement does not necessarily adversely affect the lending decision.

Conversely, bankers seem to feel strongly about accounting for leases. If leases are not capitalized, bankers request additional information and, in general, seem to succeed in obtaining it. The additional information they request is not necessarily the capitalized values of leases. They consider details about contract commitments and obligations to be adequate. Many bankers stated that they usually request a copy of each lease agreement or specific information about terms, amounts, and conditions of those obligations. Failure to comply could result in imposing more restrictive covenants, a relatively higher interest rate, or not granting the loan. A significant minority of the respondents indicated, however, that "no action" is a typical consequence.

In contrast to leases, bankers do not usually make adjustments for the omission of capitalization of interest on construction. They view that omission as being more conservative, since near-term profits would decrease by not capitalizing the interest on construction.

Finally, responses regarding deferred income taxes were mixed, and from the narrative comments, it is understood that some bankers confused deferred taxes with tax obligations.

In summary, bankers do not always require borrowers to apply all GAAP requirements in all circumstances, and they deal with loan applications in which there are GAAP departures on a case-by-case basis.

How different are private companies from public companies relative to financial reporting?

Bankers and accountants were asked to indicate their opinions about each of five propositions aimed at distinguishing between private and public companies. They expressed fundamentally different views as to whether private companies have distinctive features that should be translated into differences in accounting requirements for those companies. In particular, about 85 percent of bankers but less than 40 percent of accountants reported that:

1. The same information is needed from private and public companies for the purpose of making similar decisions.

2. Financial statements will become less useful if an accounting basis other than GAAP is used for private companies.

On the other hand, a larger percentage of accountants than bankers indicated that:

1. External users place less reliance on the financial statements of private companies than on the financial statements of public companies.
2. External users can obtain more information than is contained in financial statements from private companies than from public companies.

In general, bankers believe that information needs for decision making are similar for both types of companies. They do not seem to support different financial reporting by private companies than by public companies. In addition, both groups agreed, but with varying degrees, that private companies typically show more concern about the cost of providing financial statements than do public companies.

What measures of size should govern if private companies were to be classified as small or large?

Bankers and accountants were asked to indicate what they meant by "small." In particular, they were asked to specify the number of employees, sales in millions of dollars, and the size of total assets that they view as cutoff points for small private companies as compared to large private companies. The majority of bankers indicated that a company with total assets of $4 million or less, total sales of $4 million or less, and with 50 employees or less would be classified as a small company.

Sixty-one percent of the accountants indicated that a company with total assets of $1 million or less, with sales of $4 million or less, and with 50 or less employees would be classified as a small company. Thus accountants and bankers agreed on the cutoff points for the number of employees and the size of sales but disagreed on the cutoff point for total assets.

*Do different sized private companies adopt different
variations of GAAP?*

Bankers and accountants were asked to specify whether they require
the same applications of accounting principles for large and small
private companies. Thirty-six percent of the responding accountants
indicated differences in disclosure practices, but only 13 percent indicated that differences occur in applying accounting principles involving
measurements. Differences in disclosures were related to deferred
income taxes, pension plans, capitalization of leases, contingencies,
and outstanding debt. Differences in measurements were frequently
cited regarding capitalization of leases, deferred income taxes, and
inventory valuation.

Responses by bankers were not markedly different from responses
by accountants. About 50 percent of the bankers indicated that different sized companies provide different disclosures, but only 18 percent indicated that different sized companies use different
measurements. Furthermore, only 20 percent of the bankers stated
that they typically evaluate loan applications from each type of company differently. Finally, bankers cited "getting to know the company
managers" to be more important in making loans to small private companies than to large private companies.

How are different alternatives to GAAP perceived?

One of the alternatives explored is for maintaining the status quo,
that is, the FASB not take any action. The results reported above suggest that bankers, in particular, and many managers of private companies agree with that approach. However, a large percentage of the
accountants (excluding those from the Big Eight) disagree.

A second alternative is to modify certain accounting and reporting
pronouncements as they apply to private companies. Given that
bankers have indicated a high degree of satisfaction with the present set
of GAAP, the issue of modification was addressed in terms of the
desirability of continuing to require private companies to follow certain accounting requirements. As had been consistently reported
throughout this research, bankers and accountants strongly recommended continuing three GAAP requirements: the statement of
changes in financial position, accounting for inventories at the lower of
cost or market, and accounting for contingencies.

Bankers, in addition, indicated a strong interest in continuing the requirements for capitalization of leases, accounting for deferred income taxes, the equity method of accounting for unconsolidated subsidiaries, and accounting for pensions.

Accountants, on the other hand, do not support continuing the requirements for accounting for compensated absences and discounting long-term payables and receivables. They appear to be indifferent regarding requirements for capitalization of leases, accounting for deferred income taxes, capitalization of interest, and accounting for pensions.

A third alternative explored with accountants and managers was to create a special set of GAAP (a form of "Little GAAP") that would apply only to private companies. Both groups were asked their views of the desirability and consequences of establishing a special set of GAAP. Accountants were asked to indicate their views separately for small and large private companies. The classification of company size as to small or large was up to each respondent to define. To that extent, the responses received were perceptual. Also, those responses were to some extent hypothetical since there is no special set of GAAP available at the present time and respondents have not experienced its full consequences.

The majority of accountants indicated that a special set of GAAP would be beneficial only for the *small* private companies because it would enhance the usefulness of financial statements to the managers of those companies and would reduce the cost of applying GAAP. Furthermore, accountants did not believe that establishing a special set of GAAP for private companies would reduce the degree of accounting sophistication demanded of accountants or would reduce the cost to accountants of keeping up with developments in GAAP.

The majority of responding managers from the NAA sample indicated that a special set of GAAP would likely increase the usefulness of financial statements to outside users and managers and would reduce the cost of applying GAAP. The degree of belief indicated by managers from the random sample concerning those items was lower in magnitude than those indicated by managers from the NAA sample. With the exception of the accountants' support for creating a special set of GAAP for small companies, the stated support for a new set of generally accepted accounting principles was not strong.

Other alternatives to GAAP were explored. In a separate question, accountants were asked to specify the circumstances under which the use of the income tax basis would be acceptable in preparing the financial statements of private companies. The circumstances given to them included "use by owners only," "use by bankers," "use by suppliers," and other circumstances of their choice. Of the 330 accountants, 279 indicated that the income tax basis would be acceptable if financial statements were for use by owners only, and 140 indicated that it would be acceptable if the intended users of financial statements are bankers or suppliers. These responses are not mutually exclusive since several accountants expressed support for both situations.

Also, as a follow-up to the question about the cost of keeping up with GAAP, accountants' views were sought as to the possible means of reducing the number of hours they ought to spend to keep current. About one-third of the respondents chose the reduction of the rate at which accounting standards are promulgated, and another third chose permission to use the income tax basis without having to indicate that the basis differed from GAAP. Almost 30 percent of the accountants indicated that either of two alternatives would contribute to alleviating the problem: (a) training users of financial statements of private companies to accept modified opinions or (b) allowing accountants to deviate from certain GAAP standards for private companies without qualifying the audit opinion.

In summary, it appears that bankers want to maintain the status quo, but that they would not object strongly to abandoning the requirements of capitalization of interest on construction, accounting for compensated absences, and discounting long-term receivables and payables.

Accountants, on the other hand, indicated that enacting a special set of GAAP would be beneficial for small private companies, though they expressed views that all private companies could benefit by modifying certain accounting standards. It is not clear, however, whether the special set of GAAP that they prefer would be the income tax basis or a completely new version. The majority of accountants considered that the income tax basis would be acceptable for financial statements in circumstances in which they would be for use by owners only. However, many others believed that the income tax basis financial statements could be acceptable for use by bankers and suppliers as well. Finally, enacting a special set of GAAP was perceived to be a means by which the cost of compliance could be reduced for all private companies.

Managers presented different points of view. The managers' responses from the random sample did not seem to provide strong support for establishing a special set of GAAP, nor for making significant modifications to the existing GAAP. In contrast, the managers responding from the NAA sample stated stronger opinions that a special set of GAAP would be desirable. However, the degree of belief held by those managers was not as strong as that of the accountants, especially concerning small private companies.

Many managers expressed concern about having two sets of GAAP. Some indicated that creating a special set would only provide the accountant with "an excuse for charging higher fees because learning two sets of GAAP will cost more time." Similarly, others expressed concern that creating a special set of GAAP for private companies would make it difficult to compare their companies to others. There is the notion of being perceived as second-class citizens, which was mentioned by several other respondents. It was also clear from the responses that some managers and bankers confuse GAAP with auditing requirements to the extent that at times they commented on auditing problems when they were asked to express judgments about a special set of GAAP.

How do the responses from the Big Eight accounting firms compare with others?

Responses from 37 accountants with Big Eight accounting firms indicated general agreement, but higher consensus, with the trends and directions emerging from the results obtained from the other sample of accountants. There were a few major differences, however. The incidence of not following GAAP for certain requirements was reported to be very infrequent for small, and nonexistent for large private companies. This was the indicated response for all of the 10 accounting requirements listed, including capitalization of leases. There was near unanimous agreement, however, that accounting for leases is overly complex and not relevant to decision making by managers. The views expressed by this group concerning capitalization of leases were more negative than those expressed by the other sample of accountants. These accountants strongly questioned the need to continue requiring capitalization of leases, accounting for compensated absences, and capitalization of interest in financial reporting by private companies. The latter two accounting requirements were mentioned, not because they are perceived to be overly complex, but because of the perceived lack of relevance to decision making by outsiders and by managers.

These accountants reported a difference of less than 5 hours annually between their perception of what ought to be spent and what is actually spent on keeping current with GAAP. This represents about a 5-percent difference from what ought to be spent as compared to the 40-percent difference (37 hours) reported by the other sample of accountants.

Finally, these accountants perceived that general inflationary conditions contributed to an average of 49 percent of the increase in the practitioners' fees, while the increase in complexity and number of accounting standards was perceived to have contributed 26 percent. Both numbers are materially higher than what others perceived, but the relative relationship (of 2 to 1) between the two causes was the same.

CHAPTER 2—THE ISSUES

The Research Plan

The remainder of this report sets forth the detailed results of the research. It is organized according to the sequential steps followed in doing the research, which are summarized below.

1.	The issues: (Chapter 2)	After the existing literature was reviewed, exploratory, unstructured interviews with a small number of bankers, practitioners, and managers were conducted.
2.	Structured interviews: (Chapter 3)	Samples of bankers, practitioners, and managers were interviewed using interview guides.
3.	Survey questionnaires: (Chapter 4)	The results of the preceding steps were used in developing detailed questionnaires that, after being pretested, were sent to samples of bankers, practitioners, and managers. The responses were analyzed, contrasted, and evaluated.
4.	Follow-up interviews and statistical tests: (Chapter 5)	Samples of responding bankers and practitioners were selected according to certain criteria and were contacted by telephone. The follow-up was intended to clarify and elaborate on their written responses. Also, statistical tests were used to determine the significance of differences between averages of group responses.

Introduction

This research study examines the issues related to the application of GAAP by private companies and the possibility of allowing differences in the principles governing reporting by private and public companies. Those issues have been subsumed under terms such as "Big GAAP-Little GAAP" or "Standards Overload." A call for creating the "Big GAAP-Little GAAP" dichotomy has been repeatedly heard during recent years. It appears to be based on assumptions related to (a) the needs of financial statement users and (b) the costs of providing information. The following is an overview of the literature concerning financial reporting for private companies.

Actions of Official Committees

The potential for creating differences in financial reporting requirements on the basis of either size (small versus large) or ownership (public versus private) was recognized as early as 1952 by the American Institute of Accountants.[3] However, discussion of the issues has increased in recent years by the AICPA's formation of three special committees: in 1974, the Committee on GAAP for Smaller and/or Closely Held Businesses; in 1978, the Special Committee on Small and Medium Sized Firms; and in 1981, the Special Committee on Accounting Standards Overload.

The increasingly pressing nature of the issues is reflected in the contrast among the titles of those committees. Also, the change in focus from accounting for "the small and closely held," to the problems of "small and medium sized" firms, to "standards overload" highlights the movement toward the assertion that the problems of reporting by small and private companies are attributable to "standards overload."

The 1976 report of the Committee on GAAP for Smaller and/or Closely Held Businesses contained the following conclusions and recommendations directly related to the issues being considered (pages 8 and 9):

[Conclusions]

- . . .The same measurement principles should be applied in the general-purpose financial statements of all enti-

---

[3]American Institute of Accountants, *Changing Concepts of Business Income* (New York: Macmillan Co., 1952).

ties, because the measurement process should be independent of the nature of users and their interest in the resulting measurements.

- ... The nature of the information disclosed and the extent of detail necessary for any particular disclosure may well vary depending on the needs of users.[4]
- ... [There should be a distinction between] disclosures ... required by GAAP [and] additional or analytical [disclosures] in the financial statements of all entities.

[Recommendations]

- The Financial Accounting Standards Board should develop criteria to distinguish disclosures that should be required by GAAP ... from disclosures that merely provide additional or analytical data. ... The criteria should then be used in a formal review of disclosures presently considered to be required by GAAP and should also be considered by the Board in any new pronouncements.
- The AICPA auditing standards division should reconsider pronouncements concerning a CPA's report on (a) unaudited financial statements, including those accompanied by an "internal use only" disclaimer, (b) financial information presented on prescribed forms, and (c) interim financial statements of smaller and/or closely held businesses.
- ... The Financial Accounting Standards Board should amend APB Opinion No. 15, [*Earnings per Share*], to require only publicly traded companies ... to disclose earnings-per-share data.

The AICPA and the FASB have reacted positively to those recommendations. The Accounting and Review Services Committee (ARSC) was established to study CPA involvement with unaudited financial statements. ARSC has issued Statements on Standards for Accounting and Review Services (SSARs), which establish and delineate the CPA's involvement with unaudited financial statements of companies.

---

[4]The Committee did not directly involve users or managers in reaching this conclusion.

In 1978, the FASB added to its agenda a project on financial statements and other means of financial reporting to distinguish between information to be disclosed in financial statements and other types of financial disclosures for all companies, with particular attention to the problems of applying GAAP in reporting by small and closely held companies. In the same year, the FASB issued Statement No. 21, *Suspension of the Reporting of Earnings per Share and Segment Information by Nonpublic Enterprises,* which suspends the earnings per share and segment disclosures as requirements for reporting by private companies. In 1979, the Board issued FASB Statement No. 33, *Financial Reporting and Changing Prices,* which does not apply to private companies, and in 1980, issued FASB Statement No. 36, *Disclosure of Pension Information,* which provides flexibility for private companies in that disclosures about pension benefits and assets are required only when the information is readily available. In 1982, the FASB issued Statement No. 69, *Disclosures about Oil and Gas Producing Activities,* which exempts private companies from certain requirements.

Nonetheless, those measures do not appear to have satisfied those who have been calling for more relief. In 1980, the AICPA Special Committee on Small and Medium Sized Firms recommended that a special committee be appointed to study alternate means of providing additional relief from accounting standards that are not considered cost effective for small businesses and to study the development of another comprehensive basis of accounting. In 1982, the Technical Issues Committee of the Private Companies Practice Section of the AICPA Division for CPA Firms recommended changing or eliminating 11 accounting and disclosure requirements that the committee considered either "should not apply to private companies or do not sufficiently benefit the users of private companies' financial statements to justify their costs."[5]

Those recommendations were provided to the AICPA Special Committee on Accounting Standards Overload, which has recently released its report. In that report, the Special Committee asserts that a standards overload exists and recommends that (pages 3 and 4):

- The FASB promptly reconsider and act on certain accounting standards that are widely perceived to be

---

[5]Private Companies Practice Section, Technical Issues Committee, *Sunset Review of Accounting Principles* (New York: AICPA, 1982), p. 2.

unnecessarily burdensome and costly, particularly for small nonpublic entities.

- In reconsidering existing standards and in developing new standards, the FASB's objective should be simplification of standards by avoiding complex and detailed rules for all entities to the extent feasible.
- To the extent that simplicity and flexibility is not feasible, the FASB should explicitly and specifically consider the information needs of the users of the financial statements of small nonpublic entities and the costs and benefits of developing the information with the objective of providing, within the framework of a unified set of generally accepted accounting principles, differential disclosure alternatives . . . as well as differential measurement alternatives for such entities.

In summary, the efforts of the AICPA committees have culminated in two major strategies:

1. Identifying the problems of financial reporting by private companies as a problem of "standards overload" and
2. Transferring the problem to the FASB.

Other Research

Most of the limited research by others has addressed either specific accounting requirements or the general idea of providing differential measurement and disclosure. Arguments questioning the applicability of certain GAAP requirements to private companies generally have been based on one or more of the following assertions:

1. There are differences between the information needs of users of financial statements of public companies and users of financial statements of private companies.
2. There are differences among users regarding the degree of their reliance on financial statements of private companies as sources of information.
3. The costs of providing information are relatively higher for a private company than for a public company.

Chazen and Benson (1978) summarized the first of these grounds by asserting that financial analysts and public stockholders are the primary users of the financial statements of public companies, whereas owner-managers and creditors are the principal users of financial statements of private companies. Those different groups are then said to have different information needs. However, research results presented by San Miguel and Stephens (1982) question this implication. They reported that bank loan officers and security analysts have a high degree of similarity of preferences for various types of information that are typically included in the financial statements. They also attributed the few instances in which those two groups might have a difference in preference for information to a difference in focus (for example, cash flow analysis for bankers versus earnings per share for security analysts). In another study, Holt and Stephens (1982) reported that audit procedures used by bank examiners could affect the amounts and types of information collected by bankers. There is little else in terms of empirical evidence that clearly differentiates the information needs of security analysts from those of bankers.

Also among the research at this general level is that by Naus (1974), which summarizes the objections to having two sets of GAAP. Those objections are as follows: (a) improvements in reporting to one group of users should also result in improving the reporting to other groups; (b) all companies operate in the same environment, face similar economic conditions, and could have the same types of transactions; (c) most companies belong to either trade associations or industry groups that typically summarize financial statements of companies in the association or the group, and different accounting requirements for different companies within the same group could distort financial comparisons; and (d) many private companies would eventually become public.

Different authors have different reasons for agreeing or disagreeing with those points. Consider, for example, the discussion by McKay (1981) in which he argues for uniformity of measurements for all companies, but for allowing differences in disclosure between public and private companies. Conversely, Arnstein (1972) argues that the benefits derived from applying income tax allocation to private companies do not exceed the cost incurred. He observes that interperiod income tax allocation is misunderstood by many readers of financial statements of private companies. Arguments for suspending capitalization of leases have been advanced by Benis (1978). He postulated that investors and creditors are more interested in cash flows than in capitalized values.

A recent study by Campbell (1981) offers some interesting contrasts about bankers' use of two sets of accounting information. Campbell created two basket-type cases: a "Big GAAP" and a "Little GAAP." In the case of the "Little GAAP" package, data regarding four accounting and disclosure requirements—earnings per share, deferred income taxes, capitalized values of capital leases, and information about inflation adjustments—were excluded but could be obtained by the bankers on demand. The experiment required four bankers, two in each group, to decide whether or not to grant a loan of a specific sum to a small, closely held company. One group received the "Little GAAP" package, and one received the "Big GAAP" package. All experimental information (other than the four requirements mentioned above) was the same for each group.

In that protocol experiment, each loan officer was asked to think aloud, which enabled Campbell to obtain insights about the decision processes of the two groups. The results indicate that the bankers who received the "Little GAAP" basket did not request the omitted information concerning earnings per share, deferred taxes, or inflation adjustments. However, they either stated the need for, or requested, the information about leases. Taken at their face value, these findings lend support to the arguments advanced by those urging either modifying or rescinding certain accounting and disclosure requirements for closely held companies.

In a recent study, Nair and Rittenberg (1982) used three survey questionnaires to collect information about the views of bankers, executives of small companies, and practicing CPAs. Their samples were selected solely from the state of Wisconsin. The findings reported by Nair and Rittenberg essentially confirm that certain accounting requirements are perceived to create some difficulties, particularly for practitioners. However, on average, neither the participating bankers nor managers revealed any discernible preference for the creation of a special set of GAAP for small companies.

In a somewhat different type of study, *Inc.* magazine, which is geared to small business, conducted an extensive survey concerning small businesses and their public accountants.[6] About a 20-percent response rate provided valid responses from 993 companies and 440 practitioners. Eighty-four percent of the companies were private with sales volumes varying between $100,000 and $25 million, and 80 per-

---

[6]The results of the survey were published in a special report in the March 1982 issue of *Inc.* magazine.

cent of the accountants were either sole or local practitioners. The results of the survey include the following findings:

1. About 51 percent of the respondents regard their public accountants as their chief outside financial advisers. This was followed by their attorneys and bankers.
2. Overall, fees are not a major factor in the relationship between small companies and their accountants. Of the 10 most important factors, fees ranked number 9 while personal relations and the like were rated higher. However, the absence of a "reasonable and clear fee structure" was cited by 22 percent of the respondents as a source of major gripes between small businesses and their accountants. This was rated second to the problems with "timely service."
3. Small businesses do not make a practice of rotating their accountants. About 39 percent of the respondents report that their present accounting firm is the only one they have ever had.

Summary

The discussion presented in the preceding few pages suggests a concern about the costs relative to the benefits of applying GAAP to private companies. But the cost of applying GAAP is more easily determinable than the benefits, and therefore any analysis of the problem consists basically of statements of opinion and value judgments about the benefits. Some accountants and owners of private companies hold a strong belief that the cost of providing GAAP financial statements is too high. That belief has not been fully ascertained, however, because of the inability to measure the benefits of adopting GAAP. The AICPA committees and the several research studies that have evaluated various aspects of the problem have used various approaches—from making a reasoned value judgment to conducting a sophisticated empirical study. Yet, their conclusions point in different directions concerning the need to simplify or reconsider certain accounting standards. Prior research has not succeeded in providing support for adopting a special GAAP for business enterprises based on company size or type of ownership. Nevertheless, the debate continues unabated. For this reason, the FASB decided that several studies, including this one, should be undertaken to develop greater understanding of the underlying issues and of the merits of various possible solutions.

CHAPTER 3—ANALYSIS OF THE INTERVIEWS[7]

Introduction

Twenty-nine bankers, 18 managers of private companies, and 31 practitioners were interviewed. Those participants were affiliated with banks, companies, and public accounting firms in California, Florida, Delaware, Georgia, New Jersey, North Carolina, Ohio, and Pennsylvania. Some of them were interviewed early in the research for the purpose of identifying relevant issues, obtaining a better understanding of the environment, and developing interview guides that were tailored to each group. The interviewers used those guides in the subsequent interviews but permitted those interviewed to emphasize various points of interest. Each interviewed person also responded in writing to several questions as part of the development of the questionnaires discussed in Chapter 4.

Bankers

Bankers interviewed were commercial lending officers in banks that varied in size from $50 million to $1 billion of total assets. The number of loan applications processed by the bankers over the past 2 years varied between 25 and 300, with an average of 143 loans per banker. The bankers have been using financial statements for periods that range from 3 to 12 years.

Overall, interviewed bankers appeared to be satisfied with the existing set of GAAP. They indicated that existing disclosures are beneficial and that additional ones could be helpful. They were not interested in the prospect of having financial statements that follow the income tax basis of accounting rather than GAAP, except perhaps for very small companies. Most bankers indicated that a thorough analysis of GAAP financial statements, including the use of financial ratios and trends, greatly reduces the possibility of making a bad loan. They emphasized, however, that financial statements provide only a part of the information (and perhaps not the most important part) on which to base a credit decision. Some indicated that in only about 5 to 10 percent of

---

[7]Because the substantive results of the interviews were highly consistent with those obtained from the questionnaires reported in Chapter 4, this chapter has been substantially reduced.

their credit decisions do financial statements play a decisive role in granting credit to small companies.

The bankers had only a general idea of what accountants do in an audit or a review; some stated that a review involves as much testing as does an audit. A notable misconception of bankers (which the interviewers frequently had to explain) is the equating of GAAP financial statements with audited financial statements. The separation of duties between the managers (as the preparers of financial statements) and external auditors (as independent experts expressing an opinion on the fairness of those statements) was of relatively little interest to bankers; their primary concern was to obtain reliable information. Those bankers were asked how they would perceive the reliability of GAAP financial statements that had no involvement of an independent CPA. They considered the reliability to be similar to compilation; that is, providing much less reliability than audit or review.

The bankers believe there is no better alternative for GAAP as a basis for preparing financial statements. Most of them stated that creating a special set of GAAP for private companies would not enhance their functional analysis. To the contrary, another set of GAAP would increase their burden because of the need to decipher financial statements prepared on the basis of two sets of GAAP.

In responding to inquiries about specific areas of GAAP that are perceived to present difficulties for reporting by *small* private companies, bankers included capitalization of leases, the equity method of accounting for investment in unconsolidated subsidiaries, deferred income taxes, and discounting long-term receivables and payables.

The bankers perceived that most managers of private companies do not understand accounting specifics and rely on the recommendations of their outside CPAs regarding accounting matters. The bankers did not feel that the cost of services by an outside CPA has placed a "heavy burden" on their borrowers in many situations. They pointed out, however, that competition among banks to make loans also is a factor in obtaining information. They cannot request much additional information from their "good risk" clients without increasing the risk of losing them to competing banks. The bankers request considerably detailed information when borrowers are judged to be of "questionable risk." Some bankers indicated that, with the permission of the borrower, they address questions about the financial statements accompanying a loan application to the CPA whose name is associated with them.

Respondents provided a gross sales range of $2 to $50 million for the cutoff between companies that would be classified as small or large. Their responses were also diverse for other measures of size, such as assets and the number of employees, that could provide such a cutoff. Accordingly, no meaningful "average" size could be determined.

How important is the size of the borrowing company to the banker? Bankers were asked to rate the relative importance of 16 variables in making unsecured loans to (a) *small* private companies and (b) *large* private companies. Those variables related to the type and size of the loan, characteristics of the borrower, nature of the financial statements, and other information. The bankers gave almost identical responses for both large and small companies on each of the 16 variables with one exception: If GAAP were to be replaced in accounting for private companies, bankers were indifferent between using the tax basis and the cash basis for small companies only. This result was consistent with the assertions by all of the bankers interviewed that, in general, the *same accounting rules* should apply for large and small companies. Delineating a specific set of accounting rules for "small" companies is problematic to bankers because (a) "smallness" is a relative concept that is essentially situation specific and (b) they apply the same general criteria and techniques in accumulating and evaluating credit evidence for all the companies they deal with.

Managers

The structured interviews were with managers of relatively small companies. Although some of the companies had gross sales of about $100,000, the majority had sales that ranged from $1 million to $10 million. Most of the companies had one or more employees who maintained the accounting records, but in many cases the outside CPA used those records to prepare financial statements. The reporting periods for companies' financial statements varied from quarterly to annually with one exception.

The one exception was a wholesale company with gross sales of $10 million. It employed a full-time accountant and generated monthly financial statements. The owner-manager of that company indicated that he uses those financial statements every period to plan his decisions for the next period. According to him: "Outside accountants are too slow for my business if I ask them to prepare my monthly financial statements. . . . But the auditors come in once a year. They verify the inventory and do their tests."

Although this owner-manager gave the impression that he was pleased with the CPA services, his reasons for obtaining annual audits were stated as follows: "I really don't think it [the audit] is worth it [the fee], except to check on the honesty of my employees. The rest of it I am doing because of the Internal Revenue Service. And if I ever want to go public."

Even though the reasons given for performing audits were all related to his own uses of information as a manager, this manager indicated that the financial statements were used by "everyone I owe money to." Other managers also identified creditors as the main users of their company's financial statements.

The managers were asked why bankers might prefer GAAP as a basis for preparing financial statements. Two major factors emerged: GAAP financial statements (a) provide relevant information and (b) assist in better evaluation of the debt-paying ability of borrowers. Managers' opinions were highly variable, however, as to whether such advantages result in lower interest rates or in less restrictive covenants on loans. They rated knowing the banker and the credit history as being more important in obtaining bank loans than following GAAP or having a CPA's opinion on financial statements.

Several managers rated the cost of applying GAAP to small business as a "strong" or "very strong" reason for having a special GAAP for private companies. Specific areas of GAAP that most of them mentioned as being costly are accounting for deferred income taxes and accounting for leases. However, few managers showed much knowledge or interest in knowing the details of GAAP.

Unlike the bankers, the managers showed reasonably strong agreement with the proposition that those who make decisions about private companies generally have more ability to obtain information from the companies apart from the financial statements than do those who make decisions about public companies.

Practitioners

Most of the interviewed practitioners (not from Big Eight firms) consider the owners of private companies to be the primary users of financial statements, and bankers and credit agencies as secondary users.

Satisfaction with GAAP

The practitioners were generally satisfied with existing GAAP. They indicated, however, that the proliferation of disclosure requirements may be adding a financial burden to some clients. Additionally, practitioners in smaller CPA firms indicated that some GAAP requirements are not appropriate for small private companies. For example, some practitioners considered capitalization of leases to be a highly unreasonable standard to be required of *small* private companies.

Practitioners also indicated that owners of most small businesses for which they render accounting or auditing services find problems with specific GAAP requirements mainly because of the lack of relevance of the information for their needs. Practitioners indicated that owners most frequently mentioned capitalization of leases and deferred income taxes as problem areas. Complexity of GAAP, the cost of compliance, and high accountants' fees were three other reasons practitioners say owners give for dissatisfaction with GAAP financial statements. Practitioners indicated further that the lack of financial knowledge is another reason why business owners are dissatisfied with GAAP.

Nevertheless, practitioners believe that private companies benefit by adopting GAAP. The majority of practitioners cited reliability of information for managers' use in decision making and for use by absentee owners as one benefit. They also feel that it will assist owners in financing through debt, although the interviewees indicated that this does not necessarily result in lower borrowing costs. The practitioners perceive that a banker attributes a higher quality to GAAP financial statements in evaluating debt-paying ability of a private company because of the belief that GAAP inherently generates reliable information.

Need for Special GAAP

If the problems with GAAP are limited, what are the reasons then for a call by some for a special GAAP for small businesses? Practitioners were asked to rate the significance of possible reasons for a special GAAP and indicated the following as the main ones:

1. Current GAAP does not meet the information needs of small business managers.
2. Applying GAAP is costly for small businesses.

Practitioners indicated that owners of private companies do not have a sufficient knowledge of GAAP to request a "special" or "little" GAAP. Rather, owners are concerned about two things: the resultant financial statements and the practitioners' fees. Practitioners pointed out that owners' concern about fees has caused the practitioners to request a special set of GAAP for private companies.

Realizing that adopting any position depends on the size of the company, the practitioners indicated that a sales volume of $10 million would, on average, delineate the difference between large and small companies. The majority of them indicated that their responses concerning GAAP would be different for larger companies. Two reasons they cited frequently were the following:

1. The present set of GAAP is tailored to transactions that are more likely to occur in larger companies.
2. Larger companies are more likely to have the financial sophistication needed to develop and understand the information within the company.

Alternative Basis of Accounting

Practitioners of small CPA firms who work in smaller communities and serve private companies with a sales volume below $5 million indicated a higher use of financial statements based on either the income tax or cash basis than did practitioners involved with larger companies. In general, however, those bases were used by those practitioners much less frequently than GAAP. In most of those cases, the external CPA "prepares" the financial statements for the management. Generally though, use of those bases was infrequent.

Apparently neither the tax basis nor cash basis of accounting meets practitioners' expectations of a special set of GAAP. After having been reminded of the 1976 AICPA Statement of Auditing Standards No. 14, *Special Reports,* which permitted the use of the tax basis under certain circumstances, practitioners were asked about the reasons for its infrequent use. The majority of those interviewed agreed on three main reasons:

1. Tax basis financial statements lack credibility with lenders.
2. Practitioners do not encourage owners to use tax basis financial statements.
3. Other users besides lenders prefer GAAP financial statements.

The practitioners pointed out that the tax laws provide benefits for owners of private companies that result in a conservative measurement of income using the tax basis. Such a difference from GAAP would diminish the usefulness of financial statements for other purposes, such as the assessment of debt-paying ability.

Factors in Granting Credit

Finally, the practitioners held views similar to those of bankers with respect to the relative importance of various factors in granting credit to small private companies. The most important factors taken into account were (a) the personal knowledge of the owner-manager and (b) the credit history of the company. In fact, practitioners considered audited financial statements, compliance with GAAP, and reported appraised values of the company's assets and aged accounts receivable to be far less important than credit history or personal knowledge of managers in making the credit decision.

With respect to large private companies, practitioners considered the personal knowledge of the manager and the credit history of the company to be the two most important of the factors listed. However, they rated audited financial statements and compliance with GAAP higher for large private companies than for small private companies.

Observations

In short, two noticeable contrasts emerged from these interviews. The practitioners are not interested in adopting an alternative to GAAP whether or not such an alternative is sanctioned by standards setters. Yet, a rather strong perception of the relatively high cost of compliance with GAAP by small private companies prevailed. It appeared that exempting small private companies from certain accounting standards is the resolution preferred by many of those interviewed.

CHAPTER 4—COMPARATIVE ANALYSIS OF RESPONSES TO THE MAIL SURVEY

Introduction

This chapter presents the results of the survey of three groups involved with private companies: practitioners, managers, and bankers. Those three groups have vested interests in financial reporting through their roles as auditors (and sometimes preparers) of financial statements, preparers and internal users of financial statements, and external users of financial statements, respectively. Given the differences in the interests of the groups, a separate questionnaire was developed for each group.

This chapter first discusses the design of the questionnaires, next explains the selection of representative samples from each group, and then highlights the response profiles for each sample. The remainder of the chapter presents an analysis of the results. The analysis emphasizes the similarities and differences among responses received from all groups, as well as the uniqueness of certain issues to a particular group.

Design Considerations

The main source used to identify the concerns regarding financial reporting for private companies was the proposal for research prepared by the FASB staff with the counsel of an advisory group. That proposal discussed the substantive reporting issues for which additional information was needed. The questions considered important by that group are listed in Appendix A.

The interviews described in Chapter 3 also were helpful in designing the questionnaires, through both the verbal comments of interviewees and the field testing of several drafts of the questionnaires. Each set of questionnaires was tested with different practitioners, managers, and bankers. The final versions of those questionnaires are reproduced in Appendix B.

The use of three different questionnaires enabled each group to give special attention to issues that it considered most important and about which it was especially well qualified to provide insights. Some issues were addressed in each questionnaire, however, to enable comparisons among the three groups with respect to their experiences and perceptions. Because of the need for effective communication with each group, the precise wording sometimes varied even in questions addressing the same issue.

Exhibit 1 categorizes the issues examined in the questionnaires and indicates the extent to which common issues were addressed across questionnaires.

Exhibit 1
The Types of Issues Included in the Questionnaires

P,B	1.	Comparisons between private and public companies
P,M	2.	Identification and relative importance of different types of financial statement users
P,M	3.	Characteristics of GAAP requirements about which concerns have been expressed
		(a) Complexity of the accounting standard
		(b) Relevance of information to managers' decision making
		(c) Relevance of information to outside users such as bankers
P,B,M	4.	Advantages of using GAAP
P,B,M	5.	Advantages of using a special set of GAAP for private companies
P,B	6.	The importance of audit, review, and compilation services of outside CPAs in achieving objectives of financial statements
P,B	7.	The relative significance of accounting and auditing as opposed to other variables (such as loan size) in making the lending decision
M	8.	Cost of services by outside CPAs and the managers' assessment of the benefits received from those services
P,M	9.	The relative importance of factors that are perceived to increase the fees of outside CPAs, including the increase in accounting standards in recent years
B	10.	The types of information that bankers request when certain non-GAAP treatments are used in the financial statements of borrowers
P,B,M	11.	The degree of satisfaction with current GAAP
B	12.	The usefulness of specific non-GAAP data (for example, aging of receivables) to bankers
P,B,M	13.	Other function-related information and demographic data

P = Practitioners; B = Bankers; M = Managers

The experience and function of each group were the primary determinants in deciding which questions it would be asked. For example, information about the cost of CPA services was sought only from managers, but information about causes of increase in the practitioners' fees was requested from both managers and practitioners. No information concerning either of those two issues was elicited from bankers, since they have limited experience and knowledge in those areas. Similarly, most managers in this study were presumed to have limited, if any, management experience with public companies; thus, questions to them did not call for comparisons between private and public companies. In addition, the need to avoid unreasonable time demands on the respondents influenced the extent to which issues were addressed across groups and led to standardized response modes for most questions (with an option for the respondent to write in additional information).

Sampling Plans

Managers

Two samples of private companies were selected: a random sample and a sample of volunteers. Ordinarily, a primary benefit of using a random or representative sample is that some inference can be made to the target population.

The initial random sample consisted of 600 companies selected from the 1981 edition of the *Dun & Bradstreet Million Dollar Directory.* The absence of an exchange listing and a ticker symbol was taken as an indication that the company is not publicly held. (Further verification was obtained by asking the manager of each selected company whether the company's stock was registered with a regulatory body.) Although the sampling was random, the choice from the *Directory* was constrained by two criteria:

1. Total sales of the company must be disclosed and must be $1 million or higher.[8]

---

[8]That restriction was made for two reasons: (a) the source used for selecting the sample, *Dun & Bradstreet Million Dollar Directory,* included very few companies with sales below $1 million and (b) such companies typically look to outside CPAs for financial expertise and likely would have those CPAs respond to a questionnaire involving accounting matters.

2. The name of the president, chief financial officer, or the controller must be disclosed.

Problems in implementing those criteria reduced the initial sample size to 582. The inability to deliver all questionnaires successfully (for various reasons, such as bankruptcy) reduced the effective sample size to about 530, of which only 99 valid responses were returned. This sample of managers will be referred to as the random sample.

The second sample consisted of a self-selected group. The National Association of Accountants (NAA) requested the presidents of several NAA chapters to enlist interested members of privately held companies to respond to the questionnaire. Of the 112 who agreed to participate, 78 returned completed questionnaires. Given the selection process of this sample, the experiences and views expressed by those respondents are not necessarily representative of the population of private companies. Self-selected subjects are less likely to be neutral observers; for example, responses by participants in the self-selected sample may be representing a particular viewpoint concerning the present state of accounting. This sample of managers will be referred to hereinafter as the NAA sample. In the analysis that follows, each sample (random and NAA) is analyzed and reported separately.

Bankers

The Robert Morris Associates (RMA) supplied to the researchers a sample of 554 bankers, which consisted of the RMA representative in each of 554 commercial banks across the country. A letter from the president of RMA accompanied the questionnaire mailed to each member of the sample.

Although this sample was not completely random, its large size and geographical distribution across the 50 states ensures a high degree of representation. Since one bank loan officer came from each bank in the sample, and since banks were ranked by size, the most likely source of bias relates to bank size. To reduce this bias, the 554 banks chosen did not include the very large banks.

Practitioners

The sampling plan focused on accounting firms other than the Big Eight accounting firms. The executive directors of several state societies of CPAs were asked to provide a random sample from their current membership lists excluding those members who are with Big Eight firms. Each also was asked to provide a cover letter requesting the cooperation of the member that the researchers could include with each questionnaire.

Twelve CPA societies (Connecticut, Florida, Illinois, Indiana, Massachusetts, Michigan, Minnesota, New York, Ohio, Pennsylvania, Virginia, and Wisconsin) responded to the request. In some cases, the researchers selected the random samples from the current directory of the state society, but in most cases, the CPA society provided mailing labels for the random sample. The size of the samples was reasonably reflective of the sizes of the state societies. The smallest random sample was 30 practitioners whose names were submitted by the Indiana CPA society, and the largest was 200 practitioners selected from the directory of the New York society. In total, 1,100 practitioners from the 12 states received questionnaires. That random selection was considered to provide an adequate cross section of the "grass roots." There are no known reasons for suspecting that practitioners in other states would respond differently from those included in the sample. However, expanding the sample size and the geographical area was a contingency to be exercised if the results failed to show a reasonable degree of consensus.

Eight questionnaires also were mailed to one senior partner from each of the Big Eight firms, accompanied by a request to distribute them to practitioners involved with private companies within the firm. That sample was small because most of those firms had made their views known previously through submission of a position paper to the FASB in response to its 1981 Invitation to Comment, *Financial Reporting by Private and Small Public Companies.*

Response Profiles

Response Rates

For each of the five samples described above, the sizes and response rates are reported in Table 1. The response rates of the Big Eight sample and of the NAA sample of managers are relatively higher than the others because of the manner in which they were selected. The lowest response rate (19 percent) was for the random sample of managers of private companies and was considered satisfactory. The response rates for bankers (24 percent) and for practitioners (32 percent) are within the normal range of good response rates for such groups.

Table 1
Response Rates from All Samples

	Practitioners		Bankers	Managers	
	Big Eight	Other		(random)	(NAA)†
Initial mailing	64	1,100	554	600	112
Returns (not deliverable, etc.)	0	58	8	70	0
Effective sample	64	1,042	546	530	112
Valid responses*	37	330	129	99	72
Response rate	58%	32%	24%	19%	64%

*A few additional valid responses were received too late to include in the numbers analyzed in the study.
†This sample consisted of volunteers, hence, the higher response rate.

Profiles of Respondents' Organizations

Some of the questions requested information about the respondents' organizations. A summary of the characteristics of those organizations is presented for each group in Table 2.

Table 2
Profiles of Respondents' Organizations

Private Companies

		Percentage of Companies	
		Random Sample	NAA Sample
Total assets	$ 2 million or less	25	20
	$ 4 million or less	44	37
	$10 million or less	64	68
	$40 million or less	85	85
Sales	$ 4 million or less	16	15
	$10 million or less	33	37
	$15 million or less	49	54
	$30 million or less	60	76
	$50 million or less	71	83
Number of full-time	40 or fewer	22	4
employees	60 or fewer	37	18
	100 or fewer	53	41
	200 or fewer	61	62
	400 or fewer	72	81
Number of owners	4 or fewer	43	40
	8 or fewer	65	63
	15 or fewer	74	77
	50 or fewer	84	87
Number of managing	2 or fewer	57	44
owners	5 or fewer	87	70
	10 or fewer	96	93

Table 2 (continued)

Banks

		Percentage of Banks
Number of branches	At most 1	32
	Less than 5	54
	Less than 10	70
	Less than 20	82
Total assets	Less than $ 50 million	13
	Less than $100 million	34
	Less than $200 million	60
	Less than $400 million	72
Total time deposits	Less than $ 50 million	30
	Less than $100 million	56
	Less than $300 million	74
	Less than $400 million	83

Accounting Firms

		Percentage of Firms
Number of partners in firm	5 or fewer	70
	10 or fewer	86
	40 or fewer	90
Number of privately held client companies	40 or fewer	11
	More than 40	89
Number of publicly held client companies	5 or fewer	88
	40 or fewer	90

Those statistics provide composite profiles of the organizations having personnel who responded. However, since the information needed to construct the profiles was to be supplied by respondents, such profiles cannot be constructed of nonrespondents. Therefore, it was difficult to ascertain the extent to which respondents provided a representative sample of the population of the selected groups.

Of the 330 accounting firms represented, 231 have 5 or fewer partners, and about 90 percent of them serve more than 40 private companies but fewer than 5 publicly held companies. Hence, that sample presumably comprises practitioners most concerned with private companies.

An interesting contrast between the random sample and the NAA sample of companies is revealed by their profiles. Although both types of companies have a similar distribution of total assets and sales volume, the NAA sample of companies appears to be more labor intensive. However, only about 20 percent of those companies had less than $2 million of assets.

Although the size of companies in the random sample was randomly distributed for private companies having at least $1 million of sales, the profiles reveal that proportionately more of the relatively large companies in the sample completed the questionnaire. The reason seems to be that larger companies would generally have qualified staff to respond to the questionnaire. That reasoning also seems to apply to the NAA sample of managers. Given the method used in soliciting participation (explained earlier in this chapter), it is only reasonable to expect a higher percentage of the relatively larger companies to volunteer to complete the questionnaire.

The interviews pointed out that very small companies rely heavily on the advice of their outside CPAs (Chapter 3). Thus, companies having annual sales below $1 million would most likely have the questionnaires completed by their accounting practitioners. It would have been unreasonable to characterize responses completed in that fashion as representing managers' views.

Profiles of Individual Respondents

When asked whether they consider their companies "small" or "large," 85 percent of the managers from both samples indicated "small." Hence, the views expressed should be considered to come from those who view themselves as managing "small" companies. Those managers reported that they have been closely involved with the preparation of financial statements for an average period of 13 years. The majority (89 percent from the random sample and 67 percent from the NAA sample) considered college training to have contributed significantly to their knowledge in accounting. A slightly larger number rated their on-the-job training as an important factor in acquiring accounting knowledge.

With respect to the bankers, 11 years was the average period they had been employed as lending officers and also was the average period for being directly involved in using financial statements. While 88 percent of them indicated that college and formal training were important sources of their knowledge in accounting, they all stated that on-the-job training was also important.

Finally, the average practice experience of practitioners was 15 years. No other profile information was requested from them.

Analysis of Survey Results

The remainder of this chapter consists of analysis of the major findings generated by the responses to the survey questionnaires. The analysis presented here deals with the following issues:[9]

1. Users of financial statements
2. Satisfaction with GAAP (overall benefits of GAAP, GAAP's worth to bankers, and difficulties with certain standards)
3. Cost of GAAP (perceived causes of increases in fees charged by practitioners, cost to private companies and the perceived relationship to the benefits, perceptions of cost-benefit relationships from the bankers' viewpoint, and cost to accountants of keeping up with GAAP)
4. Homemade GAAP (extent to which practitioners[10] depart from GAAP and areas having frequent departures)
5. Financial reporting implications of perceived differences between private and public companies
6. Effects of company size on applications of GAAP
7. Perceptions of the threshold of measures that differentiate small and large companies
8. Options available for action by the FASB (perceptions about the effects and consequences of modifying GAAP or requiring a special set of GAAP for private companies)
9. Comparison of responses from practitioners in Big Eight firms with those from other practitioners.

The findings reported here are limited by the research approach used, including the characteristics of the samples selected. First, bankers were selected from the RMA's list of members, who are typi-

---

[9]The survey addressed various additional matters, including comparisons of audits, reviews, and compilations and inclusion of additional disclosures, such as aging of receivables and payables, but only those that contributed to understanding the issues of concern are reported here.

[10]Reference to practitioners does not include the responses from those in Big Eight firms. Analysis of those responses begins on p. 94.

cally from larger banks. Thus, the bankers from very small banks were not represented. Second, managers of private companies with less than $1 million of sales were not included in the mail survey because the researchers could not be sure who would be completing the questionnaires—the managers or outside accountants. Finally, questionnaires and interviews typically reflect perceptions and value judgments. Although experience shapes the formation of judgments, questionnaires are not ideal substitutes for actual data.

Also, a word of caution should be used in evaluating results in statistical terms using averages and dispersions as reported in this study. Two problems are typically associated with the use of a categorical scale. First, the meaning attributed by various respondents to a particular score (say "3" for "agree") may not be uniform. Second, the distance between two adjacent scores (for example, "2" for "disagree" and "3" for "agree") may not be equal to the distance between two other adjacent scores. Thus, the meaning of the ranking may differ from one respondent to another and from one criterion statement to another.

Users of Financial Statements

Who are the users of financial statements of private companies? This question is important because of the emphasis placed on users' information needs as the motivation for the production of accounting information. This question is especially interesting for private companies because they do not have securities traded in the public marketplace.

Of the three groups surveyed, bankers are often mentioned as one of the primary users of financial statements. However, they often lack knowledge about other users of financial statements of private companies. Hence, only managers and practitioners were asked to rank the importance that various users attach to financial statements.

Managers ranked themselves as the most important user group. As shown in Table 3, about 68 percent of responding managers from the random sample, 65 percent of responding managers from the NAA sample, and 43 percent of responding practitioners ranked managing owners as the most important user group. All three samples of respondents ranked bankers as the second most important users of financial statements of private companies. There was no agreement on the third most important user group. Managers chose suppliers, and practitioners chose absentee owners. It appears that practitioners are more aware of the information needs of managers, absentee owners, and bankers than of suppliers.

Table 3
Importance of Financial Statements
of Private Companies to User Groups

User Group	Respondent Group	Rank				
		1 %	2 %	3 %	4 %	5 %
Company management	Managers (random)	68	15	11	4	1
	Managers (NAA)	65	17	16	-	-
	Practitioners	43	20	14	12	11
Bankers	Managers (random)	23	53	20	1	-
	Managers (NAA)	28	60	11	1	-
	Practitioners	32	31	31	5	1
Suppliers	Managers (random)	3	14	31	16	-
	Managers (NAA)	15	-	54	24	7
	Practitioners	-	4	12	28	54
Bonding agencies	Managers (random)	5	4	10	11	-
	Managers (NAA)	16	26	32	16	4
	Practitioners	12	16	18	32	21
Absentee owners	Managers (random)	14	12	12	9	-
	Managers (NAA)	21	25	21	29	4
	Practitioners	14	29	26	22	9

Satisfaction with GAAP

Those involved with financial reporting often presume that GAAP is the accounting basis that should be used for all companies. Before it can be concluded that better alternatives exist, two questions must be addressed:

1. What are the perceived benefits of and problems with the existing GAAP?
2. What are the advantages or disadvantages of alternatives to GAAP?

The first question is evaluated from various perspectives in this section. Analysis of views related to the second question begins on page 93.

Overall Benefits of GAAP

Survey participants were asked to evaluate the possible effects of using GAAP financial statements. Those effects were presented as propositions (such as, adopting GAAP will lead to "lower borrowing costs," "more understandable data," and so forth) and can be grouped into three classifications:

1. *Data quality:* propositions related to relevance, reliability, and understandability of data
2. *Economic consequences:* propositions indicating that following GAAP makes it easier to finance through debt, involves lower borrowing costs, and leads to less restrictive covenants
3. *Fee information:* propositions concerning the relationship of the practitioners' fees to the benefits received.

The first classification relates to the qualitative characteristics of financial information set forth in FASB Concepts Statement No. 2, *Qualitative Characteristics of Accounting Information.* The second classification, economic consequences, was included to see if the use of GAAP financial statements is perceived to affect bankers' decisions. Finally, the question of fees also is related to the degree of satisfaction with GAAP.

Summaries of responses are reported in Tables 4 and 5 on pages 50-52. Respondents were asked to indicate, using a 5-point scale, their level of agreement or disagreement with each proposition. An examination of the frequencies presented in Table 4 reveals the following response patterns:

1. *Data quality:* Of the three groups, bankers are the most positive about the relevance and reliability of GAAP financial statements. Not less than 90 percent of responding bankers either agreed or strongly agreed that GAAP financial statements (a) provide more reliable and relevant information for managing a private company than financial statements prepared on another basis, (b) are more relevant for use by absentee owners, (c) are more reliable for use by bankers, and (d) provide more understandable data.

   In contrast, about 70 percent of responding practitioners either agreed or strongly agreed with 3 aspects of the data quality of GAAP financial statements: (a) GAAP provides more reliable information for use by bankers, (b) GAAP provides more relevant information for use by absentee owners, and (c) GAAP provides more understandable data. About half of the practitioners agreed or strongly agreed that the remaining qualitative criteria are associated with GAAP financial statements.

   The third group, managers, was divided on many of these issues. About two-thirds of them either agreed or strongly agreed that GAAP financial statements result in more understandable data. However, the managers were divided between agreement and disagreement regarding other aspects of data quality. For example, only 31 percent of the total NAA sample and 54 percent of the total random sample agreed that GAAP financial statements provide more relevant information for use by absentee owners.

2. *Economic consequences:* Opinions concerning the economic benefits of using GAAP varied. Practitioners disagreed that GAAP results in lower borrowing costs and less restrictive covenants; bankers and managers were split in their opinions. However, much more agreement within and across groups was displayed in responding to the proposition that adopting GAAP makes it easier to finance through debt. About 70 percent of both the bankers and the random sample of managers and 65 percent of the NAA managers agreed with this proposition. Only 51 percent of the practitioners shared the same view, which might in part be because practitioners are not as directly involved in making loans to private companies as are the bankers and managers of those companies.

3. *Fee information:* The majority of bankers (72 percent) and practitioners (55 percent) disagreed with the proposition that adopting GAAP results in excessive fees for the CPAs. (This particular statement was not included in the managers' questionnaire.) As to whether expected benefits to the company exceed the cost of preparing financial statements in accordance with GAAP, about 90 percent of bankers responded affirmatively, but only about 50 per-

cent of responding practitioners and managers agreed with the proposition. The difference in responses between bankers and others reflects the high confidence (even in comparison with practitioners) that bankers place in GAAP financial statements.

The above comments are supported by the levels of the means of responses reported in Table 5. On a 5-point scale (from 0 to 4), average weights given to the propositions concerning data quality are materially higher for bankers than for either practitioners or managers. Similarly, perceived effects that are expressed by consequences such as lower borrowing cost and others are rated higher by bankers than by practitioners. Also, the responses by the NAA sample of managers tended to be more negative than those made by the random sample of managers. Those findings are supported by the statistical tests of differences reported in Chapter 5.

A further indication of those relationships among responding groups is provided by the following comparison of average responses for each of the three classifications:

	Data Quality		Economic Consequences		Fee Information[11]	
	average	rank	average	rank	average	rank
Practitioners	2.60	(3)	2.10	(4)	2.34	(2)
Bankers	3.14	(1)	2.78	(2)	2.80	(1)
Managers (random)	2.97	(2)	2.84	(1)	2.30	(3)
Managers (NAA)	2.16	(4)	2.28	(3)	2.04	(4)

GAAP's Worth to Bankers

In addition to evaluating the overall perceived benefits of GAAP, bankers were asked to evaluate reasons for their preferring GAAP financial statements. Practitioners were asked to indicate their perceptions of the bankers' reasons for preferring GAAP. The possible reasons listed for preferring GAAP include permitting comparability between companies, providing more relevant information, required by bank policy, and providing an indication of a higher level of CPA involvement.

---

[11]The fee information rated here relates to proposition 8 on Tables 4 and 5. Proposition 4 concerning excessive CPA fees was excluded from this summary for comparative purposes since it was not included in the managers' questionnaire.

Table 4
Perceived Effects of Using GAAP Financial Statements

Perceived Effects	Practitioners			Bankers			Managers (random)			Managers (NAA)		
	Dis-agree	Agree	Not Sure	Dis-agree	Agree	Not Sure	Dis-agree	Agree	Not Sure	Dis-agree	Agree	Not Sure
Data quality:												
More understandable data	107	209	8	6	122	0	29	64	2	27	41	2
More relevant data for managing company	127	133	14	9	112	6	46	45	5	43	28	1
More reliable information for managing company	141	172	11	9	115	5	40	51	4	36	34	1
More relevant information for use by absentee owners	96	223	5	6	108	13	21	43	15	29	20	16
More reliable information for use by loan officers	94	222	5	2	124	2	NA	NA	NA	NA	NA	NA
Economic consequences:												
Lower borrowing cost	248	59	17	68	49	10	42	48	4	30	33	9
Less restrictive covenants	219	94	10	50	72	4	39	47	5	26	37	9
Easier to finance through debt	128	155	21	32	82	12	20	67	7	23	43	6

Table 4 (continued)

Perceived Effects	Practitioners			Bankers			Managers (random)			Managers (NAA)		
	Dis-agree	Agree	Not Sure	Dis-agree	Agree	Not Sure	Dis-agree	Agree	Not Sure	Dis-agree	Agree	Not Sure
Fee information:												
Excessive accounting fees for independent CPAs	172	139	13	79	31	15	NA	NA	NA	NA	NA	NA
Expected benefits to the company exceed the cost of preparing financial statements	151	155	20	12	104	11	33	52	11	33	31	8

Note: The category *agree* includes responses to *agree* and *strongly agree* categories. Similar additions were made for the *disagree* categories.
NA = not asked

Table 5
Perceived Effects of Using GAAP Financial Statements
(Average Responses)

Perceived Effects	Practi-tioners	Bankers	Managers (random)	(NAA)
Data quality:				
More understandable data	2.66	3.40	2.67	2.50
More relevant data for managing company	2.50	3.08	2.38	2.18
More reliable information for managing company	2.50	3.16	2.50	2.40
More relevant information for use by absentee owners	2.77	2.90	2.10	1.70
More reliable information for use by loan officers	2.77	3.53	NA	NA
Economic consequences:				
Lower borrowing cost	1.88	2.22	2.46	2.10
Less restrictive covenants	2.10	2.50	2.41	2.20
Easier to finance through debt	2.33	2.54	2.66	2.46
Fee information:				
Excessive accounting fees for independent CPAs	2.28	1.96	NA	NA
Expected benefits to the company exceed the cost of preparing financial statements	2.34	2.80	2.30	2.04

Note: The scale used here is from 0 to 4, where
    0 = unsure
    1 = strongly disagree
    2 = disagree
    3 = agree
    4 = strongly agree
    NA = not asked

A summary of responses is reported in Table 6. For each group, responses were classified in either the *strong reason, weak reason,* or *unsure* category. The *strong reason* category consists of responses indicating either *strong reason* or *very strong reason.* A similar combination was employed for the *weak reason* category. Also, average responses and degree of consensus are reported for each group.

Bankers and practitioners indicated that the following are *weak reasons* for bankers to prefer GAAP financial statements: (a) requiring GAAP is a bank policy, (b) it represents diligence on the part of bankers, and (c) it deters high risk clients. The bankers believe more strongly than practitioners that GAAP (a) provides more relevant information, (b) facilitates a better evaluation of debt-paying ability, (c) indicates a higher level of CPA involvement, and (d) permits comparability between companies.

Difficulties with Certain Standards

The degree of satisfaction with existing GAAP was pursued further by examining and comparing the views of each group concerning specific accounting standards. Based on information provided by the FASB and on findings obtained from the interviews summarized in Chapter 3, the 10 accounting standards selected for evaluation were:

1. Capitalizing leases (FASB Statement 13)
2. Capitalizing interest on construction (FASB Statement 34)
3. Accounting for deferred income taxes (APB Opinion 11)
4. Preparing statement of changes in financial position (APB Opinion 19)
5. Accounting for inventories at lower of cost or market (ARB 43)
6. Accounting for pensions (APB Opinion 8, FASB Statements 35 and 36)
7. Discounting long-term receivables and payables (APB Opinion 21)
8. Accounting for contingencies (FASB Statement 5)
9. Accounting for compensated absences (FASB Statement 43)
10. Accounting for investments in other companies on the equity basis (APB Opinion 18) (only practitioners were asked about this standard).

Table 6
Responses concerning the Reasons That Bankers Prefer GAAP Statements

Reason Given	Bankers					Practitioners				
	Number Responding			Summary Statistics		Number Responding			Summary Statistics	
	Weak Reason	Strong Reason	Not Sure	Average*	Standard Deviation*	Weak Reason	Strong Reason	Not Sure	Average	Standard Deviation
Because they provide more relevant information	14	114	1	3.23	0.68	117	207	2	2.80	0.88
Because they enable a better evaluation of debt-paying ability	17	110	2	3.15	0.70	113	211	2	2.77	0.88
Because the information is required by bank policy	87	40	2	2.14	0.96	228	96	2	2.07	0.98
Because it represents diligence by the bank loan officer	109	17	3	1.80	0.80	254	62	9	1.76	0.94
Because they indicate a higher level of CPA involvement	30	97	2	2.95	0.90	140	183	2	2.52	0.92

Table 6 (continued)

| | Bankers | | | | | Practitioners | | | | |
| | Number Responding | | | Summary Statistics | | Number Responding | | | Summary Statistics | |
Reason Given	Weak Reason	Strong Reason	Not Sure	Average*	Standard Deviation*	Weak Reason	Strong Reason	Not Sure	Average	Standard Deviation
Because they are deterrents to high risk clients	81	44	4	2.20	0.95	220	86	18	1.96	1.00
Because they permit comparability between companies	26	101	2	3.14	0.87	98	221	4	2.84	0.92

*Average and standard deviation are based on responses to a 5-point scale: 0 = not sure, 1 = very weak reason, 2 = weak reason, 3 = strong reason, 4 = very strong reason. Total responses to 1 and 2 are identified in the table as *disagree* and to 3 and 4 are identified as *agree*.

The practitioners and managers were asked to rate each of those standards regarding three characteristics: (a) overly complex, (b) relevant to decision making by managers, and (c) relevant to outside users such as bankers. Responses by 99 managers from the random sample, 72 NAA managers, and 330 practitioners were analyzed. Table 7 and Exhibits 2, 3, and 4 report the percentages of respondents agreeing with each characteristic for a given accounting standard. It should be noted, however, that managers were asked to respond only for standards that their company has applied. For example, a manager whose company has no capital leases was not to evaluate capitalization of leases. Hence, the number of managers responding to each standard was less than the full sample.

The standards can be categorized as follows:

1. *Not overly complex, but relevant:*
   a. Statement of changes in financial position
   b. Accounting for inventories at lower of cost or market
   c. Accounting for contingencies
   Practitioners and managers view those standards as not overly complex and as relevant to decision making by both managers and users.

2. *Somewhat relevant, but not overly complex:*
   a. Accounting for compensated absences
   b. Capitalization of interest on construction
   Neither of those requirements was viewed with much enthusiasm in terms of its decision-making relevance nor did many respondents indicate that it is overly complex.

3. *Overly complex, and of somewhat less relevance:*
   a. Capitalization of leases
   b. Accounting for pensions
   Capitalization of leases was rated the most overly complex among the 10 standards presented. It was clear, however, that the majority of respondents view capitalization of leases as relevant to bankers but not relevant to decision making by managers. Accounting for pensions was ranked the second most overly complex accounting requirement, and most respondents were undecided as to its relevance for managers or outside users.

4. *Not relevant, and perhaps overly complex:*
   a. Accounting for deferred income taxes
   b. Discounting long-term receivables and payables

Practitioners and managers were divided on the relevance of these two standards to managers and outside users. However, a slim majority of practitioners viewed both items as overly complex.

It is interesting to note that the percentages of practitioners that rated capitalization of leases, deferred income taxes, accounting for pensions, and discounting long-term receivables and payables as overly complex are significantly higher than the corresponding percentages for managers. Finally, the majority of practitioners view the equity method as relevant to decision making by outsiders and not overly complex.

The Cost of GAAP

For many private companies, an outside CPA provides expertise regarding accounting systems and GAAP and is heavily involved in the preparation of the financial statements. Accordingly, information about the cost aspects of the CPA's services is important in considering cost-benefit relationships involving financial reporting by private companies. Unlike public companies, private companies generally do not face statutory or regulatory financial reporting and auditing requirements (except for tax purposes). Thus, for private companies to acquire the services of outside CPAs in preparing GAAP financial statements, the perceived benefit must be at least as high as the incremental cost. Four types of information were obtained about those perceived cost-benefit relationships:

1. *Causes of increase in fees:* an assessment by both managers and practitioners of the relative contribution of each of the factors perceived to underlie increases in the fees charged by CPAs in recent years
2. *Cost-benefit relationship:* an evaluation of perceptions of managers of private companies as to the cost-benefit relationship of services rendered by outside CPAs
3. *CPA's cost of keeping up with GAAP:* a comparison of cost (in terms of time) incurred by CPAs in their efforts to keep up with the development of accounting standards
4. *Other indicators:* the cost-benefit relationships of providing financial statements for private companies compared with public companies.

Table 7
Percentages of Responses Indicating Certain Characteristics of Specific Accounting Standards

Accounting Standards	Overly Complex			Relevant to Managers' Decision Making			Relevant to Outside Users Such as Bankers		
	Prac-titioners	Managers (random)	(NAA)	Prac-titioners	Managers (random)	(NAA)	Prac-titioners	Managers (random)	(NAA)
	%	%	%	%	%	%	%	%	%
1. Capitalizing leases	76	57	73	25	33	40	52	57	71
2. Capitalizing interest on construction	38	30	34	27	31	21	33	39	32
3. Accounting for deferred income taxes	58	40	36	26	46	44	44	46	59
4. Preparing statement of changes in financial position	9	11	19	60	77	63	80	85	77
5. Accounting for inventories at lower of cost or market	10	16	9	71	81	71	77	75	69
6. Accounting for pensions	64	53	55	39	51	46	47	47	39
7. Discounting receivables and payables	55	21	32	25	45	37	39	46	46
8. Accounting for contingencies	24	26	22	50	71	58	89	80	80
9. Accounting for compensated absences	38	18	26	24	21	41	25	17	28
10. Accounting for investments based on the equity method	37	NA	NA	30	NA	NA	55	NA	NA

Exhibit 2

Percentages of Respondents Rating Specific Accounting Standards as Being "Overly Complex"

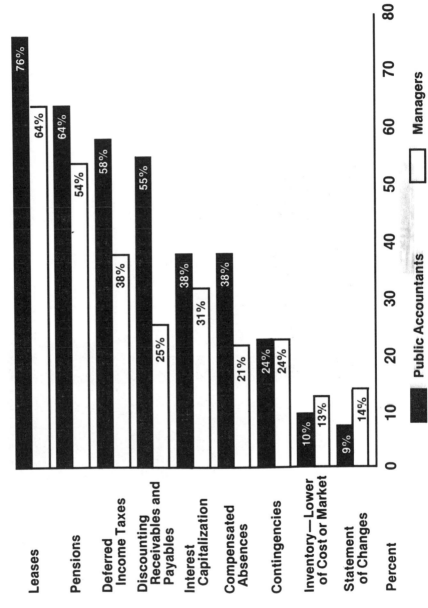

59

Exhibit 3

Percentages of Respondents Rating Specific Accounting Standards as Being "Relevant to Managers' Decision Making"

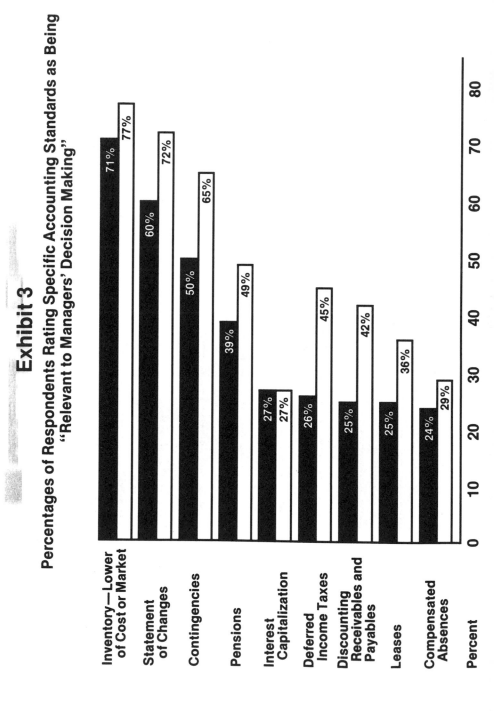

Category	Percent
Inventory—Lower of Cost or Market	71% / 77%
Statement of Changes	60% / 72%
Contingencies	50% / 65%
Pensions	39% / 49%
Interest Capitalization	27% / 27%
Deferred Income Taxes	26% / 45%
Discounting Receivables and Payables	25% / 42%
Leases	25% / 36%
Compensated Absences	24% / 29%

Percent: 0 10 20 30 40 50 60 70 80

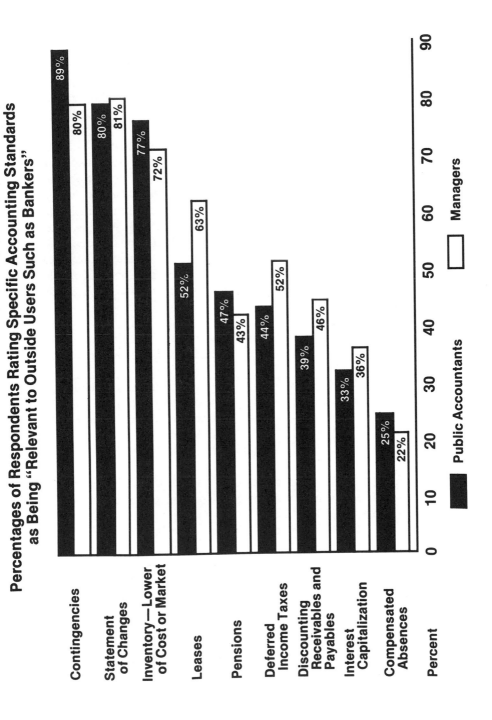

Percentages of Respondents Rating Specific Accounting Standards as Being "Relevant to Outside Users Such as Bankers"

Contingencies — Public Accountants: 89%, Managers: 80%

Statement of Changes — Public Accountants: 80%, Managers: 81%

Inventory—Lower of Cost or Market — Public Accountants: 77%, Managers: 72%

Leases — Public Accountants: 52%, Managers: 63%

Pensions — Public Accountants: 47%, Managers: 43%

Deferred Income Taxes — Public Accountants: 44%, Managers: 52%

Discounting Receivables and Payables — Public Accountants: 39%, Managers: 46%

Interest Capitalization — Public Accountants: 33%, Managers: 36%

Compensated Absences — Public Accountants: 25%, Managers: 22%

Percent

■ Public Accountants   □ Managers

61

The factors leading to increased fees by CPAs can be viewed from different viewpoints. From a standard-setting point of view, those factors consist of two categories: those that *are* controlled by standards-setting bodies, and those that *are not* controlled by standards-setting bodies.

Both categories of factors were considered in the study by Nair and Rittenberg (1981) referred to in Chapter 2. In that study, two samples of Wisconsin practitioners and managers of small private and public companies provided different rankings of those factors. Managers rated the increase in accounting standards as the fourth most important reason for the increase in the fees of the outside CPAs, whereas practitioners rated it second only to general inflationary conditions.

With the findings of Nair and Rittenberg in mind, this research sought responses from both managers and practitioners about causal links between the following five factors and recent increases in CPAs' fees:

1.	Controlled by standards-setting bodies:	(a)	The increase in volume and complexity of accounting standards
2.	Not controlled by standards-setting bodies:	(b)	General inflationary conditions
		(c)	Better internal reporting
		(d)	Increase in business volume and transactions
		(e)	Other factors

Each practitioner and manager was asked to allocate 100 points to those 5 factors, indicating the perceived degree of importance of each to increases in CPAs' fees.

The researchers viewed each factor as possibly being positively correlated with changes in CPAs' fees. For example, inflation would tend to cause increased fees. Similarly, an increase in volume and complexity of accounting standards should result in CPAs spending more time in auditing or accounting for certain transactions and charging higher fees. This positive relationship, however, is not as self-evident for the factor "better internal reporting." It can be argued that better internal reporting should facilitate the audit, review, or compilation. However, for small private companies it is not unusual for outside CPAs to perform most of the accounting services required by their clients. Hence, the fees of outside CPAs could have been increasing due to extending their services for the purpose of improving the internal accounting system. Thus it was not clear that the relationship between the factor of better internal reporting and the increase in fees of outside CPAs would necessarily indicate a positive correlation.

The results of the responses to this question by practitioners and managers are reported in Table 8 and Exhibit 5. In summary:

1. On average, practitioners and managers are consistent in their rankings of the five factors that are thought to contribute to the increase in CPAs' fees.
2. General inflationary conditions were perceived to have caused between an average of 37 percent (practitioners' responses) and 41 percent (managers' responses) of the increase in the fees charged by outside CPAs. However, practitioners appear to show greater agreement with respect to this causal factor than do the managers.
3. On average, increase in accounting standards (in terms of both complexity and number) was rated second only to general inflationary conditions by both practitioners and managers. It was perceived to have caused an average of 21 percent to 24 percent of increase in the fees of outside CPAs. Practitioners again showed a higher degree of consensus.
4. Increase in business volume and transactions was perceived to have caused an average of 17 to 19 percent of increase in fees charged by outside CPAs. For the fourth important factor, better internal reporting, managers from the random sample attributed 8 percent of increases; NAA managers indicated an average of 12 percent; and practitioners attributed about 13 percent. It should be noted, however, that little agreement among respondents is revealed for both of these factors.

Perceived Cost-Benefit Relationship

Managers were asked their views of the cost of the CPAs' services compared to the benefits received. This issue was approached in two ways. In the direct approach, managers ranked the perceived cost-benefit relationship. In the indirect approach, managers indicated their tolerance regarding increases in fees charged by CPAs.

Table 8
Relative Weights of Perceived Causes of the Increase in Fees for Services Charged by Outside CPAs As Viewed by Practitioners and Managers

Perceived Cause	Practitioners Percentage		Managers (random) Percentage		Managers (NAA) Percentage	
	Average Weight	Dispersion of Responses*	Average Weight	Dispersion of Responses	Average Weight	Dispersion of Responses
1. General inflationary conditions	37	21	40	26	41	30
2. Better internal reporting	13	12	8	13	12	17
3. Increase in accounting standards (complexity and number)	24	17	21	19	23	20
4. Increase in business volume and transactions	17	14	19	19	18	17
5. Other factors	5	11	4	10	5	10
6. Rounding errors and missing responses	4	—	8	—	1	
Total points	100		100		100	

*Dispersion gives an indication of consensus. High dispersion means low consensus.

Exhibit 5

Perceived Causes of the Increase in Fees for Services Charged by Outside CPAs

Perceived Cause

1. General inflationary conditions
2. Increase in complexity and number of accounting standards
3. Increase in business volume and transactions
4. Better internal reporting
5. Other factors
6. No response

Percent

	Public Accountants	Managers—random	Managers—NAA
1.	37%	40%	41%
2.	24%	21%	23%
3.	17%	19%	18%
4.	13%	8%	12%
5.	5%	4%	
6.	4%	8%	5%
			1%

Direct approach

Managers were asked the following question:

For the benefits provided by the CPA firm to your company, the fees charged were (please circle one):

| Much too low | Too low | About right | Too high | Much too high |

Responses to this question are tabulated in Table 9. It is perhaps not surprising that no one indicated that the fees were *much too low* for the benefits provided. Only about four percent of the respondents perceived the fees to be *much too high* for the benefits received. Over half of the responses indicated that fees were *about right,* but slightly less than one half indicated *too high.*

Table 9
Responses to the Question,
"For the Benefits Provided by the CPA Firm
to Your Company, the Fees Charged Were":

| Possible Responses | Responding Managers | | | |
| | Random Sample | | NAA Sample | |
	Number	%	Number	%
Much too low	0	0	0	0
Too low	1	1	0	0
About right	52	54	38	54
Too high	40	42	28	40
Much too high	3	3	4	6
Total	96	100	70	100

Why did a large number indicate that the fees were *too high*? Possibilities include: (a) it might be a reflection of the actual situation or (b) it could be a "rational" reaction of individuals who, as most rational decision makers do, prefer more benefits for less cost. Narrative comments by respondents did not provide insights about those possibilities. Nevertheless, in light of prior findings that managers perceive certain accounting standards to be unduly complex, it seems likely that some of them do in fact believe the cost is *too high* in relationship to the benefits received from the services of outside CPAs.

Indirect approach

Managers were asked indirectly about their satisfaction with the fees they are currently paying outside CPAs. They were requested to state the level of fee increase at which they would become so dissatisfied that they would change accounting firms. A summary of responses is reported in Table 10.

Both samples of managers responded similarly. The majority of responses were clustered at the level below the 30-percent category for increase in fees, and the average response was about 24 percent. This percentage suggests that, on average, respondents will become extremely dissatisfied if the fees charged by outside CPAs increase by 24 percent.

Table 10
Percentage of Fee Increase That
Would Result in Changing CPAs

Percentage Increases	Responding Managers			
	Random Sample		NAA Sample	
	Number	%	Number	%
0 – 10%	8	9	4	6
15%	14	16	10	15
20%	26	29	18	26
25%	16	18	20	30
30%	10	11	1	1
35%	5	5	8	12
40%	1	1	1	1
45%	10	11	2	3
50%	0	0	4	6
Total	90	100	68	100
Average	25%		24%	

Another aspect of the cost of GAAP is the time demands placed on CPAs to keep up with GAAP. Many practitioners view the time that they spend studying new pronouncements as time taken away from other opportunities. It is possible, therefore, that the perceived opportunity cost, not the technical content of new standards, underlies those symptoms generally ascribed to "standards overload." The approach used to examine that possibility is again indirect because of its sensitivity and of limitations inherent in eliciting information by means of mail questionnaires.

Practitioners were asked to estimate the number of *hours per year* they believe a practicing CPA must devote to remain current with GAAP. They were then asked to indicate the number of hours per year that a practitioner in a firm of the same size as theirs spends in trying to keep current with GAAP. The two questions were asked in an indirect mode in order to avoid negative reactions associated with intrusive or personal questions. Furthermore, the number of hours per year appeared to be as good a surrogate of the CPA's opportunity cost as any other.

Responses to the two questions indicate that the opportunity cost is perceived to be material. The 317 responding practitioners estimated that an average of 91 hours per year is needed to keep current with GAAP, assuming the current rate of promulgating financial accounting standards. They estimated that an average of 54 hours was being spent annually. That is, keeping up with GAAP would require a practitioner to spend, on average, about 70 percent more time than what is actually spent studying accounting standards.

The 317 responses had high variations among them. The variation within the "ought to be" responses was 85 hours and within the "actual hours spent" responses was 50 hours. The differences between the average hours of what ought to be spent and of what is spent are statistically significant, suggesting that some of the responding practitioners do not devote the time necessary to keep up with current developments in GAAP. The reasons for their failing to do what they themselves perceived as ought to be done cannot be clearly delineated; the opportunity cost argument is only one of many possible explanations. This study does not provide sufficient basis for speculating about the reasons.

The cost-benefit relationship also was addressed in other parts of the survey. Practitioners were asked to evaluate the proposition that the cost of providing financial statements is relatively greater for private than for public companies. Similarly, bankers were asked if their private company customers show relatively greater concern about cost than their public company customers.

About 89 percent of the bankers either strongly agreed or agreed with the proposition that private companies are more concerned with the cost of providing financial statements than are public companies. Sixty-five percent of the practitioners either strongly agreed or agreed with the proposition that the cost of providing financial statements is relatively greater for private companies. In short, both bankers and practitioners agreed, but with varying degrees of conviction, that providing financial statements is more costly for private companies than for public companies.

Another comparison of cost benefit can be gleaned from responses to the statement: "Expected benefits to the company exceed the cost of preparing financial statements," which was evaluated by all groups (bankers, managers, and practitioners). The proposition was part of a question concerning the accounting basis used in financial reporting and the characteristics claimed to be associated with using GAAP. Relative frequencies (percentages) of agreeing or disagreeing with that proposition are summarized in Table 11. As shown, more managers of the random sample (54 percent), as compared with the NAA sample (43 percent), agree or strongly agree that the expected benefits of providing GAAP financial statements by private companies exceed the cost of providing them. Practitioners are evenly divided between agreeing (47 percent) and disagreeing (47 percent). The majority of bankers agree (64 percent) or strongly agree (17 percent) with the expected benefits of using GAAP. This is another example of bankers showing greater enthusiasm about benefits of GAAP than do managers and practitioners.

Homemade GAAP: Manifestation of Difficulties

As indicated previously, many practitioners expressed concern that certain accounting requirements are overly complex and of questionable relevance to either managers or bankers. Although practitioners are not alone in expressing this concern, practitioners were more

Table 11
Responses to the Proposition That
Expected Benefits of Adopting GAAP Exceed the Cost

	Practitioners		Bankers		Managers (random)		Managers (NAA)	
	Number	%	Number	%	Number	%	Number	%
Strongly agree	30	9	22	17	11	11	3	4
Agree	122	38	82	64	41	43	28	39
Disagree	122	38	11	9	23	24	18	25
Strongly disagree	29	9	1	1	10	11	15	21
Not sure	20	6	11	9	11	11	8	11
Total	323	100	127	100	96	100	72	100

inclined than managers to view certain accounting standards as overly complex. This is illustrated in Table 7 for (a) capitalization of leases, (b) accounting for pensions, (c) accounting for deferred income taxes, and (d) discounting receivables and payables. In addition, as was reported earlier (Table 4), a majority of practitioners and bankers believe that the costs of providing financial statements are relatively greater for private than for public companies. These views are important in that they may have an impact upon financial reporting practices.

The perceived standards overload and the findings of Nair and Rittenberg (discussed in Chapter 2) indicate frequent incidences of departures from GAAP, which suggest a need to evaluate how frequently and in what areas practitioners elect to depart from GAAP. If different practitioners elect not to follow GAAP for specific but different accounting requirements, then in effect they are creating their own brand of "Little GAAP." Information on how frequently the responding practitioner has elected to depart from GAAP was requested for each of the 10 accounting standards that practitioners evaluated in terms of their complexity and relevance. Responses were elicited separately for large and small private companies, with the definition of small and large being left to the individual respondent. This approach was adopted after efforts to delineate quantitative measures of company size were not successful because what is considered a "small company" for some is a "large company" for others. Responses to the question on departing from standards are summarized in Table 12. Four observations can be made about that table:

1. Not all of the 330 practitioners completing the questionnaire chose to respond to this question. As shown, the number of respondents varied from 103 to 194, depending on the accounting standard for which information was requested.
2. The number of respondents who indicated a high percentage of departure from various standards is significantly greater for the small than for the large companies. That is, more of the respondents indicated that the departures are made more frequently for the small than for the large private companies.
3. The least frequent departures were reported for the standards that practitioners had rated earlier as both relevant and not overly complex: inventory valuation, the statement of changes in financial position, and accounting for contingencies.
4. The most frequent departure, especially for small private companies, occurs for those standards that practitioners had described

Table 12
Number of Practitioners Indicating That Certain Accounting Standards
Were Not Followed for a Percentage of Private Company Clients

Accounting Standard	Company Size	Total Number of Responses	Number of Responses Indicating 100% of Time	Percentage Distribution of Respondents Indicating Level of Frequency of Not Following Standard				Average % of Time Not Followed
				Highly Infrequent	Infrequent	Frequent	Highly Frequent	
1. Capitalization of leases	S	194	35	49	17	8	26	44
	L	133	6	81	6	3	10	19
2. Capitalization of interest	S	132	33	50	18	3	29	42
	L	103	11	78	7	0	15	20
3. Accounting for deferred income taxes	S	188	38	45	22	4	29	44
	L	133	8	75	15	3	7	19
4. Inventory valuation at lower of cost or market	S	154	8	68	19	5	8	24
	L	113	2	87	9	0	4	10
5. Accounting for pensions	S	159	35	46	22	4	28	43
	L	119	14	74	12	0	14	22
6. Investment in related companies	S	142	24	55	20	4	21	36
	L	118	7	77	15	0	8	18
7. Accounting for contingencies	S	153	14	52	24	6	18	37
	L	116	5	77	12	3	8	19
8. Accounting for compensated absences	S	183	85	21	17	7	55	70
	L	142	45	40	21	3	36	50
9. Statement of changes in financial position	S	168	4	72	14	7	7	22
	L	115	7	92	3	3	2	2
10. Discounting receivables and payables	S	159	85	28	12	3	57	66
	L	127	52	43	10	5	42	53

Note: The frequency of not following standard in: below 25 percent of the time — highly infrequent;

earlier as not being relevant to managers or to outsiders: accounting for compensated absences and discounting interest on receivables and payables.

The earlier responses regarding complexity and relevance and the frequency of departures from standards in items (3) and (4) above are related. To provide further evidence about this relationship, practitioners were asked to rank three possible reasons for departures from the standards: (a) lack of relevance to owners, (b) too costly, and (c) consistency with the accounting basis used. The last reason was included to allow for responses relating to the preparation of financial statements on a basis other than GAAP. The results of this rating are reported in Table 13. A number of those who responded to the question concerning departure from standards did not state their reasons for doing so. (This difference can be noted by comparing the numbers of respondents in Table 12 with those in Table 13.)

For most standards, either relevance of information to owners or concern for cost was the motivating force in departing from GAAP. This conclusion is supported by a comparison of the responses of those rating cost or relevance and those rating consistency with the accounting basis as primary reasons for departing from standards.

The data presented in Table 13 may be summarized as follows:

1. On average, relevance to owners and concern for cost were cited three times more frequently than consistency with the accounting basis as reasons for departures.
2. Relevance to owners was the primary reason for electing not to follow standards for discounting receivables and payables, capitalization of leases, capitalization of interest, and for accounting for investments in related companies.
3. Cost, on the other hand, appears to be the primary reason for not preparing the statement of changes in financial position and for not following standards in accounting for pensions and compensated absences.
4. Not capitalizing leases appears to be motivated by both cost and lack of relevance to owners.
5. Finally, all three reasons appear to be equally important for not following standards for contingencies, inventory valuation, and accounting for deferred income taxes.

Table 13
Summary of Rank Ordering of Relative Importance of Reasons for Electing Not to Follow GAAP

Accounting Requirement	Number of Practitioners Responding to This Question*	Response		
		More Relevant to Owners	Less Costly	Consistent with the Particular Accounting Basis Used
		% Rating It First	% Rating It First	% Rating It First
1. Capitalization of leases	155	43	38	19
2. Capitalization of interest on construction	97	44	22	34
3. Accounting for deferred income taxes	137	39	31	30
4. Inventory valuation	100	32	32	36
5. Accounting for pensions	109	30	46	24
6. Investment in related companies	99	53	29	18
7. Accounting for contingencies	104	39	33	28
8. Compensated absences	151	27	42	31
9. Statement of changes in financial position	97	29	59	12
10. Discounting receivables and payables	131	49	28	23

*Number of practitioners responding varied and not all of the respondents (330) considered responding to this question.

The research did not produce hard evidence as to whether deviations from standards were always accompanied by qualified opinions. However, some rather "soft" evidence is reported in Chapter 5 concerning additional results.

The consequences of those departures are of interest. If different versions of homemade GAAP are being followed, what actions do bankers typically take when the financial statements of borrowers are based on those versions? That question was addressed to bankers with respect to four different standards:

1. Capitalization of leases
2. Accounting for deferred income taxes
3. The statement of changes in financial position
4. Capitalization of interest on construction.

For each of those standards, bankers were asked to indicate:

1. The frequency with which they encountered departures
2. The types of additional information they typically request when they encounter departures
3. How frequently they receive that information
4. If the requested information is not received, the frequency of (a) adding more restrictive covenants, (b) increasing the cost of granting debt, (c) reducing the size of loan from what the borrower had requested, (d) taking other actions (to be individually specified by the respondent), and (e) taking no particular action.

Table 14 summarizes the frequencies with which the bankers encountered departures and received additional information they requested for each of the four standards. Table 15 summarizes the actions that bankers indicated they typically take as a result of not receiving the information.

As shown, of the four standards, the most frequently encountered departure is the omission of the statement of changes in financial position. On a 7-point scale (where 1 is most infrequent and 7 is most frequent), the average response for the frequency of omitting the statement of changes in financial position is 3.9. However, on a 5-point scale, the average of the frequency of positive reactions to bankers' requests for the statement was very high (3.59 out of 5 points maximum). Both responses indicate a high degree of consensus. Ironically,

Table 14
The Frequency of Bankers Encountering Deviations from Certain Standards and Degree of Success in Obtaining Additional Information Requested

Event	Total Responses*	Average†	Degree of Consensus‡
1. Capital Leases:			
a. Not capitalized	124	2.51	low
b. Additional information was received	102	3.27	high
2. Interest on Construction:			
a. Not capitalized	120	2.15	very low
b. Additional information was received	69	2.64	high
3. Deferred Income Taxes:			
a. Not accounted for	122	2.64	high
b. Additional information was received	84	2.30	very high
4. Statement of Changes in Financial Position:			
a. Not prepared	124	3.90	very high
b. Additional information was received	92	3.59	very high

*Bankers responding to item (a) and not to item (b) either did not request additional information or requested but did not receive information.

†A 7-point scale ranging from highly frequently (7) to highly infrequently (1) was used for item (a), and a 5-point scale ranging from highly frequently (5) to highly infrequently (1) was used for item (b).

‡Consensus here is measured by coefficient of variation (variance/mean) because the scale was not consistent throughout. The higher the coefficient of variation, the lower the consensus.

Table 15

The Types and Frequency of Actions Taken by Bankers

When Requested Information Was Not Received

Information requested about:	Total Responses	Number of Those Indicating Taking Action When Requested Information Was Not Received				
		Add More Covenants	Increase Interest Rate	Reduce Size of Loan	Other	No Action
1. Capital leases	106	42	4	1	14	45
2. Interest on construction	73	19	0	6	15	33
3. Deferred income taxes	77	28	1	6	21	21
4. Statement of changes in financial position	87	23	0	1	27	36

preparing the statement of changes in financial position was described by practitioners and managers as not overly complex and as somewhat more relevant in decision making by both bankers and managers. Although practitioners (Table 12) indicated that the omission of the statement of changes in financial position is highly infrequent, according to the bankers responding to this questionnaire, the incidence of this omission is relatively common. Furthermore, a relatively large proportion of bankers (36 out of 87) indicated that they typically take no action if the statement of changes in financial position has not been presented. A similarly large proportion of bankers stated that they prepare the statement of changes themselves. Some typical comments from bankers were "If financial statements are sufficiently detailed, the statement could be created"; or "We construct our own statement in the bank."

Several respondents (23 out of 87) indicated that the absence of a statement of changes in financial position leads to the imposition of additional restrictive covenants. A general comment by some of the respondents was "Omission of statement would indicate a lack of financial sophistication. I would expect other strengths to be demonstrated." Another typical comment was somewhat noncommittal: "It all depends on the situation." Those comments reveal the relatively high degree of professional judgment (beyond examining certain financial information) that bankers retain.

Responses by bankers suggested a relatively low frequency of encountering departures from the standard for accounting for leases (average 2.51 out of a maximum of 7 points, but with widely dispersed responses). Nonetheless, most of those bankers requesting additional information about leases indicated success in obtaining it. This is evidenced by an average response of 3.27 out of a maximum of 5 points with a relatively high degree of consensus among respondents. In addition, a significant number of bankers (42 out of 106) in this case indicated that more restrictive covenants could result from failure to comply with requests for additional information. However, an almost equal number of bankers stated that typically they take no action. A "no action" response was often accompanied by statements such as "require capitalization in the future." The bankers indicated that they typically request additional information if leases are not capitalized, but the nature of the information they ask for varies considerably from one banker to another. Many stated that they usually request a copy of each lease agreement and more specific data such as terms, amounts, conditions, and dates of future obligations. Failure to comply with those requests might result in "increasing the margin of safety," "questioning the reliability of other accounting treatments," or taking some other action, which is very much "a function of the total financial picture and of the individual loan structure."

The accounting standard that generated the least controversy is capitalization of interest. Most bankers stated that no adjustment is needed if interest is not capitalized on construction. This view was shared even by those who stated that they typically request additional information. A significant number of bankers indicated interest in finding out specific information about the terms of debt used to finance construction because "knowing the percentage of interest attributable to construction is helpful in evaluating operating profits." The responses of some bankers suggested to us a lack of understanding of this accounting standard.

The responses that bankers gave when deferred income taxes are not accounted for are similar to those they gave concerning the omission of capitalization of interest. The typical information bankers request consists of the tax return or amounts and reasons for nondisclosure and the calculation of deferred income taxes. Some bankers (28) indicated that failure to comply with requests for information may result in adding more restrictive covenants; a smaller number (21) indicated that typically no action is taken. Those stating "no action" typically conditioned that statement on a general remark, such as "It depends on the situation." Twenty-one respondents indicated they usually take "other actions." Those actions varied from possibly denying a loan to requiring the client to make tax payments at the bank.

In summary, it appears that bankers face situations in which departures from GAAP occur with relatively high frequency. Two general observations follow from their reactions to those situations:

1. Bankers do not always obtain additional information when they request it after observing deviations from GAAP. But when the omitted information is considered crucial for evaluating the risk of the borrower, they either acquire the information before making decisions or provide for some other safeguards, such as additional restrictions.

2. When the omitted information is not considered crucial for the assessment of risk of the client or if it can be generated internally by bankers, either bankers do not request that information from the borrower, or bankers take no action (adverse to the borrower) when they do not receive the requested information. Hence, in

some instances, bankers may be considered acquiescent with respect to applications of some versions of homemade GAAP.

Comparing Private and Public Companies

By design, this study focuses on financial reporting by private companies. However, since practitioners and bankers deal with both public and private companies, the question arises as to the differentiating characteristics of both types of companies and the implications of those characteristics for financial reporting. This issue was addressed in the questionnaires of both practitioners and bankers. In each questionnaire, respondents indicated the extent of their agreement or disagreement on a 5-point scale to each of five statements about the differentiating characteristics of public and private companies. Table 16 presents two types of summaries for each of the five statements: (a) the frequency of agreement or disagreement with the statements and (b) the mean and standard deviations of responses. The response scale was reduced to three categories: *at least agree* (representing the responses indicating either *agree* or *strongly agree*), *at least disagree* (representing responses to either *disagree* or *strongly disagree*), and *unsure.*

As shown, relatively more bankers than practitioners agreed with three of the statements. By comparison with public companies,

1. Financial statements would be less useful if private companies account for their activities differently.
2. The same information is needed from private companies for making similar decisions.
3. Private companies show more concern for the cost of providing financial statements.

Relatively more practitioners than bankers were in agreement with the remaining two statements. By comparison with public companies,

4. Less reliance is placed on the financial statements of private companies.
5. More information can be obtained on request from private companies.

Also, bankers consistently show a higher level of agreement among themselves than do practitioners. The only exception is that bankers

80

disagreed more among themselves than did the practitioners regarding the proposition that bankers could easily obtain more information from private companies than from public companies.

In summary, practitioners' responses appear to view private companies as having distinctive features that should affect financial reporting. Bankers, on the other hand, do not share that view. In particular, bankers generally do not see a strong basis for supporting differential treatments of financial reporting by private companies. The only distinctive characteristic about which a large majority of both practitioners and bankers were in agreement is that private companies show more concern about the cost of providing financial statement information. One other earlier finding is supported: bankers are not always as successful in obtaining information on request from private companies as outsiders are led to believe.

Effects of Company Size

Bankers and practitioners were asked to indicate whether they require the same level of information disclosures and application of the same accounting principles from small and large private companies.

In some respects, responses to those issues highlight differences in the perceptions about the distinctions and trade-offs between disclosure and measurement. While 36 percent of the responding practitioners indicated that small and large private companies do not provide the same level of disclosure in financial statements, only 13 percent stated that different accounting principles (measurements) are generally followed in preparing the financial statements of each type of company. When asked to elaborate, practitioners indicated that differences in disclosures between small and large private companies are generally related to deferred income taxes, pension plans, leases, contingencies, and debt structure. Differences in the application of accounting principles frequently relate to capitalization of leases, deferred income taxes, and inventory valuation.

Bankers responded differently. While about 50 percent of them expected different disclosures between small and large private companies, only 20 percent stated that they typically evaluate loan applications from each type of company differently. To bankers, the disclosure differences between small and large private companies center on the following issues:

Table 16
Responses by Bankers and Practitioners concerning Comparisons between Public and Private Companies

	Frequency				Average		Dispersion	
	Practitioners		Bankers		Practi-tioners	Bankers	Practi-tioners	Bankers
	Disagree	Agree	Disagree	Agree				
1. Although most private companies have fewer or simpler activities than do most public companies, they cannot account for those activities differently without making the financial statements less useful to you.	196	124	23	99	2.25	2.86	1.00	0.83
2. When you make decisions about private companies, you typically need the same information as when you make decisions about public companies.	208	118	17	109	2.25	3.14	0.91	0.63
3. When you make decisions about private companies, you generally rely less on financial statements of those companies than when you make decisions about public companies.	118	207	78	46	2.65	2.20	0.92	0.83
4. You generally are able to obtain more information (beyond that reported in financial statements) from private client companies than from public client companies.	58	266	43	79	3.07	2.64	0.81	0.95
5. Your private client companies show more concern about the cost of providing financial statements than do your public client companies.	90	214	9	113	2.70	3.20	1.11	0.88

Note: The following scale was given for responses:

0 = unsure   3 = agree

1 = strongly disagree   4 = strongly agree

1. While insisting on audited financial statements for large companies, bankers stated that they frequently accept reviewed financial statements for small private companies. Although occasionally accepted, compilations are viewed by bankers as undesirable and generally misleading.
2. The amount of information that is disclosed by small private companies is generally less than what is disclosed by large private companies. As some respondents put it, for the small companies, "disclosure is limited to those items needed to fully assess cash flow and debt service."
3. Several bankers have noted that disclosures by small private companies are defective in connection with one or more of the following: deferred income taxes, leases, contingencies, and debt structure.
4. Although most bankers indicated that small private companies would not be expected to provide as much disclosure as large private companies, getting to know the management and understanding the companies' plans were considered more vital for small companies. (It should be noted that many of the responses were made as a mixture between what is expected and what is actually reported by the small and large private companies.)

Whereas 50 percent of the responding bankers indicated that different sized companies do in fact provide different financial disclosures, only 18 percent of them expected differences in the application of accounting principles (measurements). In other words, about 82 percent of the responding bankers stated that they expect small and large private companies to follow the same accounting principles. This contrast provides insights about bankers' preferences for information. While bankers have persistently asked that all companies follow GAAP (regardless of size or type of ownership), the pattern of responses reported above suggests that, when asked about GAAP, bankers think of accounting *measurements*. It further suggests that bankers might tolerate differences in disclosure requirements for small and large private companies but would find it difficult to tolerate differences in measurements.

Perceptions of Measures of "Small" Company

As previously stated, the majority of practitioners indicated a preference for establishing a special set of GAAP for small private companies. Although the researchers have not been able to devise a measure of size that would be generally acceptable, company size plays a major role in determining the attitudes and preferences toward the application of GAAP. Thus, it is necessary to achieve some understanding of the measures of size that respondents in all three groups had in mind for small companies when they responded to the questionnaires.

As a follow-up to the question concerning effects of company size, bankers and practitioners were asked to indicate the levels of different factors that they use to classify private companies as either large or small: total sales, total assets, number of employees, and number of persons employed by the client company as internal accountants.

Based on the pretesting and the interviews that were conducted, the questions regarding size were designed for response only by those who indicated that different sized companies should follow different methods either for disclosure or for accounting principles. Accordingly, only 110 practitioners and 47 bankers responded to those questions. The results obtained are summarized in Table 17.

Several observations can be gleaned from this table. First, about 60 percent of the practitioners who responded to this question indicated that they would classify a company as small if its total assets are $1 million or less, but only 38 percent of the bankers agreed with that threshold. However, responses were more similar for sales. About 60 percent of bankers and practitioners would classify a private company as small if net sales are below $4 million. With respect to the number of employees, for about 60 to 70 percent of bankers and practitioners who responded to this question, 50 employees or less would result in classifying a company as small.

Table 17
Respondents' Views of Thresholds for Small Companies*

	Percentage of Responses from	
	Bankers	**Practitioners**
Number of Employees:		
20 or fewer	28	24
20 to 50	44	36
more than 50	28	40
Sales in Million Dollars:		
one or less	30	40
1.0 to 4.0	27	20
4.0 to 10.0	32	33
greater than 10.0	11	7
Total Assets in Million Dollars:		
one or less	38	61
1.0 to 4.0	43	16
4.0 to 10.0	6	18
greater than 10.0	13	5

*Bankers and practitioners were asked to provide measures that, in their views, delineate "small" and "large" companies.

The Options Available for Action

Of the several possible courses of action by the FASB concerning financial reporting by private companies, three were evaluated in the survey questionnaire and are discussed here. The first is that GAAP remain essentially the same for private and public companies. For example, this could embrace simplification of GAAP for all companies. The second option entails modification of the present set of GAAP when applied to financial reporting by private companies. That modification might take any of several forms, including differential measurement, differential disclosures, or both. Finally, the third option is the possibility of creating a new set of GAAP that would apply only to private companies.

Information about maintaining one set of GAAP for all companies was obtained by eliciting information concerning the perceived benefits of GAAP, the extent of satisfaction with GAAP, and the relationship to the cost of applying GAAP. The preceding analysis has presented that information. The other two options are considered in this section.

The Case for Modifying GAAP

Certain accounting standards appear to be more problematic for private companies than are others. Although bankers, practitioners, and managers of private companies share some of the perceptions about the complexity of certain accounting standards, they do not agree on the relevance for decision making of the information resulting from the application of those standards. Of the three groups, bankers are the most satisfied with the present GAAP and the least interested in making changes. However, a direct assessment of the difference between the attitudes of bankers and other groups could not be made from the analyses reported above. The extent to which GAAP should continue to be required was the subject of another question for the practitioners and for the bankers. Both groups were asked to indicate the level of agreement or disagreement with the proposition that each of 10 accounting standards should continue to be required of private companies. The 10 accounting standards included are those for which complexity and relevance to decision making were examined. Admittedly, practitioners' responses would be based on their perceptions of the bankers' role, but they should serve as a way of evaluating how practitioners perceive the role of accounting in loan decisions.

Responses for each of the standards were recorded on a 5-point scale ranging from strongly agree to strongly disagree. The summary of responses in Table 18 indicates that both bankers and practitioners agree that the following three standards should continue to be required for private companies:

1. The statement of changes in financial position
2. Accounting for inventories at lower of cost or market
3. Accounting for contingencies.

Those are the same three standards the participants evaluated as highly relevant for decision making by managers and by bankers. Also, as before, bankers agreed more among themselves than did practitioners.

Bankers and practitioners expressed more divergent views about the remaining seven accounting standards. Bankers, for example, want private companies to continue following the standards for capitalization of leases, accounting for deferred income taxes and, to a lesser degree, the equity method and accounting for pensions. Practitioners disagreed with continuing the standards for accounting for compensated absences and discounting payables and receivables. Practitioners appeared to be indifferent regarding the remaining standards. If part of the support by bankers was due to their enthusiasm about GAAP generally, it may be that bankers and practitioners hold similar views concerning accounting for compensated absences, interest on receivables and payables, and capitalization of interest on construction.

It should be noted that the question addressed to bankers referred to small private companies, whereas the question to practitioners referred to private companies without the qualifying description *small.* Although that inconsistency was not intentional, it could have biased bankers' responses relative to practitioners' responses regarding continuation of standards for private companies. However, bankers indicated that 7 of the 10 accounting standards should continue to be required for financial reporting by small private companies. If the question had not been qualified by the descriptive *small,* bankers presumably would have expressed even stronger support for those standards than presented in Table 18.

Table 18
Responses by Bankers and Practitioners
concerning the Need to Continue Requiring
Certain Standards for Private Companies

Standard	Practitioners Average*	Practitioners Dispersion†	Bankers Average	Bankers Dispersion
1. Capitalization of interest	2.28	1.03	2.52	1.09
2. Capitalization of leases	2.26	1.02	3.13	0.68
3. Accounting for deferred income taxes	2.43	1.04	3.15	0.68
4. The equity method	2.44	1.03	2.90	0.98
5. Preparing statement of changes in financial position	3.11	0.98	3.34	0.71
6. Accounting for inventories at lower of cost or market	3.21	0.85	3.30	0.75
7. Discounting payables and receivables	1.97	0.98	2.55	1.11
8. Accounting for compensated absences	1.98	0.98	2.19	1.14
9. Accounting for contingencies	2.80	1.01	3.20	0.72
10. Accounting for pensions	2.30	1.01	2.80	1.06

Note: The response scale is from 0 to 4, where
  0 = unsure
  1 = strongly disagree
  2 = disagree
  3 = agree
  4 = strongly agree

---

*Average indicates level.
†Dispersion indicates the degree of consensus. The higher the dispersion, the lower the consensus.

Creating a new set of GAAP that would apply only to private companies is another option open to standards setters concerning financial reporting by private companies. Whether or not this special set of GAAP is what others have called "Little GAAP" is not a relevant issue. Rather, the issue is whether a special set of GAAP for private companies would indeed change such characteristics of the present GAAP as the quality and relevance of financial statement information and the cost of applying GAAP.

Given the way that bankers feel about existing GAAP, it would have been superfluous to elicit their views concerning a significant deviation from the present system. Thus, questions concerning cost and expected usefulness of enacting a special set of GAAP for private companies were addressed only to managers and practitioners.

A summary of responses to both questions is reported in Tables 19 and 20. Average responses and the degree of consensus are reported in Table 19. Practitioners were given the choice to respond for both small and large private companies because, unlike managers, practitioners express their views in relation to their practice in total. Although we had initially searched for a quantitative measure for company size, we could not find a single measure with which most participants agree. As a result, company size was categorized simply into small and large. That classification permitted each practitioner to respond to small and large according to what is relevant to his or her operations. However, individual responses for small or large companies obviously varied depending on the definition each had for that classification. To that extent, the results obtained only indicate leanings rather than very precise evaluations of attitudes and perceptions.

About 325 of the 330 practitioners completed the section on the small companies. The number for the large companies was slightly lower (it varied from 300 to 312 depending on the statement). Practitioners were relatively consistent in indicating that a special set of GAAP would (a) reduce the cost of applying GAAP and (b) enhance the usefulness of financial statements to company managers. This consistency was higher for the responses related to small companies. Similarly, practitioners disagree with the propositions that a special set of GAAP would (a) reduce the degree of accounting sophistication demanded of CPAs and (b) reduce the cost to the CPA of keeping up with developments in GAAP.

Table 19
Responses to Possible Benefits of a Special Set of
GAAP for Private Companies—Averages and Dispersion

Expected Benefits of Having a Special GAAP	Managers (random) Average*	Dispersion†	Managers (NAA) Average	Dispersion	Practitioners Size	Average	Dispersion
1. Would increase usefulness to outside users	2.10	1.27	2.32	1.16	S L	2.30 2.02	1.13 1.10
2. Would reduce degree of accounting sophistication demanded of CPA firms	2.16	1.10	1.94	1.07	S L	2.00 1.76	1.10 1.00
3. Would reduce the CPA's cost of knowing GAAP	2.00	1.12	1.73	0.84	S L	1.90 1.70	1.01 0.94
4. Would reduce accounting sophistication expected of managers	2.30	1.02	2.26	0.96	S L	2.60 2.30	1.00 0.93
5. Would enhance usefulness of financial statements to managers	2.50	1.21	2.75	1.14	S L	2.93 2.66	1.10 1.09
6. Would reduce cost of applying GAAP	2.60	1.27	2.51	1.12	S L	3.14 2.81	1.00 1.04
Number of respondents	99		72			226	

Note: The response scale is from 0 to 4, where
   0 = not sure   3 = strong reason
   1 = very weak reason   4 = very strong reason
   2 = weak reason   S = small company; L = large company

*Average indicates level.

Table 20
Responses to Possible Benefits of a Special Set of GAAP—Agree or Disagree

A Special Set of GAAP for Private Companies Would:	Managers (random)		Managers (NAA)		Practitioners			
					Small Companies		Large Companies	
	Disagree	Agree	Disagree	Agree	Disagree	Agree	Disagree	Agree
1. Increase usefulness of financial statements to outside users	45%	42%	38%	51%	52%	44%	62%	33%
2. Reduce degree of accounting sophistication demanded of CPA firms	57%	33%	70%	23%	68%	32%	76%	22%
3. Reduce cost to the CPA of keeping up with GAAP	57%	34%	83%	14%	72%	27%	80%	18%
4. Reduce degree of accounting sophistication demanded of managers	60%	36%	57%	42%	40%	59%	57%	41%
5. Enhance usefulness of financial statements to managers	34%	57%	29%	67%	28%	71%	35%	62%
6. Reduce the cost of applying GAAP	29%	59%	40%	54%	20%	79%	31%	68%

Note: Percentages do not add to 100 percent because the responses to the category *unsure* were not tabulated above. Number of practitioners responding to this question for small companies is 325, but only 312 responded for large companies.

Practitioners responded differently for the small and large private companies when they were asked to assess the increase in the usefulness to outside users of financial statements prepared under a special set of GAAP. The majority of respondents either disagreed or were uncertain whether a special set of GAAP would enhance the usefulness of financial reports to outside users. Practitioners' responses in this case reflect both a divided opinion and a higher uncertainty about the impact of a special set of GAAP on small private companies. On the other hand, 62 percent of the practitioners disagreed with the proposition related to large companies; that is, in their opinion, enacting a special set of GAAP would not enhance the usefulness of financial statements of large private companies.

The remaining item with which practitioners made differing responses according to the company size is the degree of accounting sophistication demanded of the managers of private companies. A slight majority indicated that enacting a special GAAP would reduce the degree of accounting sophistication demanded of the managers of small private companies, but only 41 percent of the respondents agreed with this proposition for large private companies. In brief, practitioners were generally supportive of the view that enacting a special set of GAAP would reduce the cost of applying GAAP and would enhance the usefulness of financial statements to managers, especially in the case of small private companies.

Compared with practitioners, managers indicated relatively less agreement about the usefulness of a special set of GAAP for private companies. Furthermore, whereas practitioners stated a strong view that a special set of GAAP would enhance the usefulness of financial statements to managers and would reduce the cost of applying GAAP, managers' responses are somewhat weaker.

Managers also disagreed that enacting a special set of GAAP is likely to reduce the CPA's cost of keeping up with GAAP or reduce the level of accounting sophistication needed by the CPA. On the other hand, they believe that a special set of GAAP is likely to increase the usefulness of financial statements to outside users. Additional statistical tests of responses are reported in Chapter 5.

Thus far, two approaches have been discussed: either electing to develop a special set of GAAP for private companies or to selectively modify certain accounting standards for those companies. Comparing the results obtained for each of those two approaches clearly indicates that practitioners prefer to have a special set of GAAP enacted for financial reporting by *small* private companies, while the managers of those companies prefer a selective modification of certain accounting standards. Consequently, it becomes important to know what practitioners mean by "small" when referring to company size.

Other Alternatives

An obvious alternative to GAAP, and one that has been considered a serious contender, is the income tax basis of accounting. In a separate question, practitioners were asked to specify the circumstances under which the use of the tax basis in preparing the financial statements of private companies would be acceptable. The following three situations were provided: (a) by owners only, (b) by bankers for secured loans, or (c) by suppliers. In addition, respondents were given the opportunity to write in other circumstances. The responses to this question are as follows:

Circumstances	No. of Responses
Owner use only	279
Use by banker	140
Use by suppliers	139
Other circumstances	76

Many of the 330 responding practitioners marked more than 1 circumstance under which they view the use of the tax basis acceptable. In their response to this question, practitioners favor the application of the income tax basis in preparing the financial statements of private companies *if the intended users are the owners only.* A substantial number of them (about 40 percent of the respondents), however, would be willing to extend this view if the financial statements were intended for use by either owners or creditors.

Other approaches for reducing the perceived difficulty with applying GAAP to private companies may not call for a new set of GAAP. In another question, practitioners were asked to state the conditions that would lead to reducing the number of hours CPAs ought to spend on keeping current with GAAP. Given the response to the choices provided, the adoption of an alternative to GAAP and the need to reduce the rate at which accounting standards are promulgated were equally preferable. The responses received from the 330 practitioners were as follows:

1. One hundred twenty-six for reducing the rate at which accounting standards are promulgated

2. One hundred sixteen for permitting other accounting bases for private companies (such as the income tax basis) without opinion qualification
3. Ninety-three for training users of financial statements of private companies to accept disclaimers and qualified opinions for specific deviations from GAAP
4. Ninety-seven for allowing individual practitioners to deviate from certain GAAP standards for private companies without qualifying the audit opinion.

The total number (432) is greater than the 330 respondents because several marked more than 1 choice. This pattern indicates that a significant number of practicing CPAs *implicitly* believe that the problems related to financial reporting by private companies is multifaceted: it is not only a matter of standards overload, but it is also a problem with the users' lack of acceptance of financial statements that are accompanied by qualified audit opinions.

Responses from Practitioners in Big Eight Firms

As indicated earlier, eight questionnaires were sent to a senior partner in each of the Big Eight CPA firms with a request to have them completed by practitioners that deal with private companies. Thirty-seven valid responses were received by the specified time. This presents a brief discussion of the results obtained in the form of comparison with the results of the other sample of practitioners.

As did the other sample of practitioners, the Big Eight practitioners indicated that managers and bankers are primary users of financial statements of private companies. Unlike the results of the other sample of practitioners, however, they rated absentee owners slightly higher than managers.

Also, consistent with responses of the other sample of practitioners, three accounting standards were rated as not complex and as highly relevant to managers and bankers: (a) the statement of changes in financial position, (b) accounting for inventories at lower of cost or market, and (c) accounting for contingencies. The opinions of the Big Eight respondents concerning those three standards were much stronger than those of the other practitioners. For example, between 33 and 37 out of 37 respondents shared the above view.

Similarly, Big Eight respondents considered capitalization of leases to be the most complex (32 out of 37) and the least relevant to decision making by managers (32 considered it irrelevant), but they were divided concerning the usefulness to bankers. Next to leases, they considered accounting for deferred income taxes and pensions as overly complex and generally not relevant to decision making, especially by managers. They also believe that capitalization of interest and accounting for compensated absences lack relevance to decision making, although they consider neither to be overly complex.

Of significance, however, is that departure from GAAP is reported to be very infrequent; the highest frequency reported was less than 10 percent of the time and was reported for the areas of capitalization of leases and accounting for compensated absences for small private companies. Both of those accounting requirements plus capitalization of interest scored very low on the list of the accounting standards that respondents believe should continue to be required by GAAP for reporting by private companies. Nevertheless, they perceived the benefits of GAAP to lie more in the qualitative characteristics of the reported data: relevance to absentee owners and bankers and more understandability of the data. Respondents agreed on only one of the economic consequences: the relative ease of financing through debt. They also perceived relevance in evaluating debt-paying ability to underlie bankers' preference for GAAP financial statements.

The benefits of enacting a special set of GAAP for private companies were reported to lie in three areas: (a) reducing the cost of applying GAAP, (b) enhancing the usefulness of financial statements to management, and (c) reducing the degree of accounting sophistication required of managers. Respondents' scores rating agreement with these three propositions were higher for the small as compared with the large private companies.

Two further deviations from the results reported earlier for the other sample of practitioners are observed, and both relate to the cost of GAAP. Higher percentages of the increase in CPAs' fees were attributed to general inflationary conditions (49 percent) and to the increase in complexity and number of accounting standards (26 percent). Improving internal reporting received only a 6 percent weight for the Big Eight practitioners.

The second deviation from the other results lies in the cost to the CPA of keeping current with GAAP. The respondents indicated that an average of 109 hours per person ought to be spent annually to keep current, while an average 104 hours were actually spent. The difference (of about 5 hours a year) between what is perceived to be necessary and what is estimated to be actually spent is much smaller than the difference of 37 hours reported by the other sample of practitioners.

A further contrast between results is in the area of comparing private and public companies. Practitioners of both samples agreed with two propositions: (a) decision makers can obtain more information from private companies on request and (b) the cost of providing GAAP is perceived to be higher for private companies; however, practitioners in the random sample agreed more with (a) than with (b).

Finally, there was high agreement that either sales or total assets of about $4 million represent the threshold between small and large companies.

CHAPTER 5—ADDITIONAL EVIDENCE

Additional evidence concerning issues under consideration is presented in this chapter. This evidence consists of (a) feedback from follow-up interviews with practitioners and bankers to obtain additional information about certain findings from the questionnaire survey and (b) statistical tests of certain results from that survey.

Follow-up Interviews

Practitioners

A random sample of 22 practitioners was selected from those whose completed questionnaires indicated at least occasional departures from GAAP for certain accounting requirements. The follow-up interviews, which were carried out by telephone, focused on three issues: (a) reasons for departing from GAAP, (b) reasons for not spending enough time to keep current with GAAP, and (c) rating of audits, reviews, and compilations.

The questions that were asked and the responses are summarized below. (Certain practitioners provided more than one answer to a question.)

Q1. Relating to your response to Question 3 of the mail survey, what was the reason for your choosing not to follow GAAP? What was the rationale? Did you call attention to it in your report?

Comments	Number of Responses
We qualify opinions	1
Item was not material based on its magnitude	4
Item was not material because it didn't make a difference to the user	4
Item was not relevant to users' needs	4
Statements were for internal use only	3
GAAP was too costly	5
For interim report only	1

Q2. Relating to your responses to parts (a) and (b) of Question 13 in the mail survey, why is there a difference between hours a practitioner must devote to remain current with GAAP, and hours that a practitioner spends?

Most of the 22 practitioners used continuing professional education (CPE) requirements as a benchmark for the time spent to keep current. Most indicated that they spend a little more time than is required for CPE. Others indicated that specialists in their firm spend more than 80 hours a year, but not everyone could spend that much time.

Q3. When bankers appraise the reliability and quality of audits, reviews, and compilations, they tend to rate reviews as being nearly as good as audits. When CPAs make the same rating, they place reviews with compilations. Can you offer any insights into the different perspectives?

Comments	Number of Responses
Bankers accept reviews if inventory is not material	1
The bankers do not know the difference	7
The bankers place more assurance than is warranted in reviews	3
The bankers were correct in that there is more involvement by the CPA in reviews and audits than in compilations	4
No thoughts	5
Other factors	3

Bankers

In responding to the questionnaire survey, bankers showed little divergence in views. That high degree of consensus on various issues motivated the use of another sample of bankers for the follow-up interviews by telephone. The objective was to validate certain results obtained through the questionnaire and to obtain information on the extent to which bankers tolerate qualified audit opinions.

Fifteen bankers in Ohio, Pennsylvania, and Delaware were asked a series of questions. The 10 Ohio bankers were asked a specific set of questions, and the results of those interviews are summarized below. However, the responses of the five bankers from Pennsylvania and Delaware were consistent with those from Ohio, especially with respect to the views on the acceptability of qualified audit opinions. Given that no great inconsistency with earlier findings resulted from those interviews, no additional telephone interviews were made.

Q1. What do you do when audit opinions are qualified because of accounting?

Comments	Number of Responses
Don't make loan	1
Get further information	9

Q2. What do you do when financial statements are based on GAAP with one exception for which the audit opinion was qualified?

Comments	Number of Responses
Get more information depending on qualification	10

Q3. What do you do when audit opinions are qualified due to:

	Responses			
	Obtain More Information	Prefer Not Capitalized	Foot-note†	Haven't Seen
Deferred income taxes not recorded	10			
Capitalized leases declared not recorded	8		2	
Interest on construction not capitalized	8	2*		
Compensated absences not accrued	7	1	2	
Contingencies are stated but not measured	8		1	1

*Preference is because failure to capitalize is more conservative.
†Footnote is acceptable because bank adjustment (even if subjective) can be made.

Q4. How much is an acceptable trade-off between disclosure and measurements in financial statements?

Comments	Number of Responses
Prefer measurement on financial statements	3
Full disclosure is acceptable, but muddies the situation	5
Disclosure is acceptable if complete	2

Q5. Why don't you insist on obtaining the information you requested?

Comments	Number of Responses
I always receive it	5
Usually receive it, but exception is made based on judgment	3
Competition may intervene	2

Q6. How much weight do you place on credit history and character of borrower as compared to financial statements?

Comments	Number of Responses
75% to 25%	1
Credit history and character of borrower greater	3
Equal	5
Situation specific, depending on type of credit	1

In brief, qualified opinions do not appear to constitute an automatic trigger for penalizing the borrower; a majority of the 10 Ohio bankers indicated that it all depends on the nature of the qualification. This is essentially the same view as that of the Delaware and Pennsylvania bankers contacted for the follow-up interviews.

Statistical Tests

Chapter 4 did not elaborate on the statistical tests performed on the survey data. Because some of those tests provide useful results, they are presented in this section for completeness and for appreciation of the insights they provide.

The statistical tests followed two approaches: (a) making evaluative classifications of responses and (b) using student t-statistics. Both methods were used to test the significance of differences between averages of group responses regarding (a) the perceived benefits of adopting GAAP in financial statements for private companies (Question 14 of the practitioners', 7 of the bankers', and 6 of the managers' questionnaires), (b) the perceived worth of GAAP to bankers (Question 11 of the practitioners' and 4 of the bankers' questionnaires), and (c) the perceived benefits of promulgating a special set of GAAP (Question 5 of the practitioners' and 4 of the managers' questionnaires).

The Evaluative Classification

Each of the questions mentioned above included several propositions or criteria for which responses were requested. Responses to those propositions or criteria were used to evaluate attitudes toward the matter addressed by that question. For example, the propositions relating to the perceived benefits of GAAP focused on borrowing costs, reliability of data, and so on. Each response to a proposition or criterion was ranked using a 5-point scale (for example, strongly agree, agree, not sure, disagree, strongly disagree).

Two problems are typically associated with the use of that type of categorical scale. First, the meaning attributed by various respondents to a particular score (say "3" for "agree") may not be uniform. Second, the distance between two adjacent scores (for example, "2" for "disagree" and "3" for "agree") may not be equal to the distance between two other adjacent scores. Thus, the meaning of the ranking may differ from one respondent to another and from one criterion statement to another.

As a way of dealing with those problems, an evaluative approach was adopted. In that approach, the responses of each individual to all the criteria statements in a given question are examined as a unit. Based on the pattern of responses to various criteria statements of the same question, each of three coauthors (acting as judges) separately classified the individual's attitude toward the subject matter addressed by that question as favorable, neutral, or unfavorable. The ratings provided were then compared for consistency among the three judges (inter-rater reliability). Consistency checks (using the Phi correlation coefficients) were made for the classifications of each question by sample. Because inter-rater reliability was very high, classification averages for the three judges were used in comparing the attitudes of various groups to a given subject matter.

The Parametric Test

Another way of comparing responses of different groups to a given question makes use of student t-tests. Since this test for differences is a parametric test,[12] care is required in applying it to data generated from responses made on a predetermined scale. In this case, the scores provided by a given respondent to the criteria statements of a given question were aggregated to form an index. To generate more meaningful indexes, summing up of response scores should be "signed" in the sense that marking a score of "strongly disagree" to a negative criterion statement should be added as favorable, and marking "strongly agree" to a negative statement should be added as unfavorable. The criteria statements were designed so that all response modes are of the same direction. Thus, in obtaining indexes, the problem of "signing" the scores in view of the type of response did not arise.

Each respondent to a given question has an index for that question representing the sum of the weights given to the criteria statements describing the issue being addressed in the question. A practitioner responding to question 14, for example, could have an index of 30 if he or she marked the score "agree" to each of the 10 criteria statements in that question. Given the bounds of the scale (from 0 to 4), the minimum possible index is 0, whereas the maximum is 40. In general, the index for this 5-point scale is bounded from below by zero and from above by four times the number of criteria statements.

The indexes of a particular question were averaged for each group (sample). Given the relatively large samples of all groups except those from the Big Eight, the average for each group other than the Big Eight should be normally distributed (by the central limit theorem) with a mean and a variance estimated by the samples' mean and variances. The estimated mean and variances were then used to test the significance of the differences between average indexes of different samples.

This analysis is also subject to the limitations of attributions of meaning and distance equality as discussed above. However, the value

---

[12]The use of parametric statistics requires making assumptions about the properties of probability distributions of data.

of a statistical analysis of this type lies in its consistency with the categorical analysis discussed above.

The Results

The test results using both approaches were generally consistent. Accordingly, the tests using t-statistics are not presented here. The highlight of some results using the evaluative categorization tests follows.

Frequency distributions of the evaluative classifications of responses were compared; chi-squares were generated to test the significance of differences between distributions.

The classification of response patterns of bankers and practitioners concerning the perceived benefits of GAAP as "favorable," "neutral," and "unfavorable" is presented in Table S-1. That classification is the average result of all three judges. The chi-square value (at the bottom of the table) indicates a high degree of significance. That is, the distribution of responses are statistically different between practitioners and bankers. That conclusion is directly apparent from the frequencies of responses, which show that 33 percent of practitioners' responses compared with only 4 percent of the bankers' responses were classified as "unfavorable."

Table S-1
Classification of Response Patterns concerning
the Perceived Benefits of GAAP—Bankers and Practitioners

	Practitioners Other Than Big Eight		Bankers	
	No.	%	No.	%
Favorable	158	50	112	89
Neutral	53	17	10	8
Unfavorable	104	33	4	3
Total	315	100	126	100

Note: These classifications are the averages of those made by the judges. The chi-square statistic is 50.2, which indicates statistically significant different distributions between bankers and practitioners at a probability level below 0.001.

The three-way classification of response patterns of bankers and practitioners concerning the perceived worth of GAAP to bankers is reported in Table S-2. As the percentages of "unfavorable" classification indicate (42 percent for practitioners and 12 percent for bankers), the response patterns are clearly significantly different. That is further confirmed by the high value of chi-square reported at the bottom of the table. The results in Tables S-1 and S-2 are consistent with those of the t-tests: bankers attribute significantly higher benefits to GAAP than do practitioners.

Table S-2
Classification of Response Patterns concerning
the Perceived Worth of GAAP to Bankers

| | Practitioners Other Than Big Eight | | Bankers | |
	No.	%	No.	%
Favorable	143	45	91	72
Neutral	42	13	20	16
Unfavorable	131	42	15	12
Total	316	100	126	100

Note: The classifications are the averages of those made by the judges. The chi-square statistic is 36.4, which indicates that the distributions are statistically different at a probability level below 0.001.

Evaluation of the expected usefulness of a special set of GAAP is summarized in Table S-3 on page 106. The distributions of response patterns for practitioners are significantly different for small private companies than for large ones; 46 percent of the practitioners look favorably upon creating a special GAAP for small as compared to 30 percent for large private companies. The chi-square value confirms the statistical significance of that difference.

Similarly, there were statistically significant differences between the responses of practitioners for the large private companies and the responses of each of the managers' samples. (Managers were not asked to delineate specific responses between small and large private companies.) That pattern indicates that relatively more practitioners than managers do not favor the creation of a special GAAP for the large private companies. This is one of the few results that is different from that reported by the t-statistics above. The comparison of practitioners for the small private companies with the randomly selected managers shows a statistical significance at 0.05, but the comparison with the responses of the NAA managers does not reveal significant differences.

In summary, the results of the evaluative classification comparisons regarding expected usefulness of a special set of GAAP were generally consistent with those reported by the t-tests, with minor exceptions. Those exceptions are (a) the classifications of practitioners' responses to expected usefulness of GAAP for small private companies were not different from the classifications of managers' responses and (b) the reverse was true for the response concerning the expected usefulness for the large private companies. It is more likely that those exceptions are caused by the distortion introduced by having an added filter (the judges' own perceptions) of the responses of participants.

A further summary of the results of these tests is presented in Tables S-4 and S-5. Table S-4 is concerned with the directional comparison of perceived satisfaction with the present set of GAAP, while Table S-5 reports the comparisons of expected usefulness of a special set of GAAP as viewed by different groups. These results were essentially the same for the various tests performed.

Table S-3
Classification of the Responses to the
Expected Usefulness of Special Set of GAAP

	Practitioners Other Than Big Eight				Managers (random)		Managers (NAA)	
	Small Companies		Large Companies					
	No.	%	No.	%	No.	%	No.	%
Favorable	143	46	91	30	38	39	30	40
Neutral	61	19	59	19	28	28	19	25
Unfavorable	110	35	153	51	33	33	26	35
Total	317	100	303	100	99	100	75	100

Note: The classifications are the averages of those made by the judges. The chi-square statistics are as follows:

19.3, for the difference between practitioners – large and small;

8.2, for the difference between practitioners – large and random sample of managers;

6.8, for the difference between practitioners – large and the NAA sample of managers;

all of the above are statistically *significant* at a probability level below 0.01;

3.9, between the practitioners – small and the random sample of managers (statistically significant at 0.05);

1.6, between the practitioners – small and the NAA sample of managers.

Table S-4
A Summary of the Relationships
of Levels of Satisfaction with GAAP

Groups	Bankers	Practitioners (not Big Eight)	Managers (random)	Managers (NAA)	Practitioners (Big Eight)
Bankers (B)	—	B > P	B > RM	B > NM	B > E
Practitioners (P) (not Big Eight)	P < B	—	P = RM	P > NM	P = E
Managers (RM)	RM < B	RM = P	—	RM = NM	PM = E
Managers (NM)	NM < B	NM < P	NM = RM	—	NM < E
Practitioners (E) (Big Eight)	E < B	E = P	E = RM	E > NM	—

The symbol ">" means significantly better.
The symbol "<" means significantly worse.
The symbol " = " means not significantly different.

Table S-5
Summary of Test Relationships of Index of
Expected Usefulness of Special GAAP

		Managers		Practitioners			
		Random	NAA	PS	PL	ES	EL
Managers	(RM)	—	nd	RM < PS	nd	nd	nd
	(NM)	nd	—	NM < PS	NM > PL	nd	NM > EL
Practitioners	(PS)	PS > RM	PS > NM	—	PS > PL	nt	nt
	(PL)	nd	PL < NM	PL < PS	—	nt	nt
Practitioners	(ES)	nd	nd	nt	nt	—	ES > EL
	(EL)	nd	EL < NM	nt	nt	EL < ES	—

"<" means significantly less than.
">" means significantly greater than.
nd = not significantly different.
nt = not tested.
P = practitioners not including Big Eight.
E = practitioners from Big Eight.
S = responses for small companies.
L = responses for large companies.
RM = random managers.
NM = NAA managers.

Appendix A[13]

AREAS FOR WHICH FACTS ARE NEEDED

1. What characteristics of a company determine if it is a "small business" for financial reporting?
2. Who uses the financial statements of smaller privately owned businesses? Are those users different from those for large publicly owned businesses? If yes, how?
3. What factors have affected the information needs of various users of financial statements of smaller privately owned businesses and how? For example, for lenders, what impact have factors such as the following had on information needs and uses:

   a. Type of loan (for example, secured versus unsecured)
   b. Characteristics of company (for example, size and legal form)
   c. Existing knowledge about the company and its management
   d. Ability to obtain information from sources other than financial statements.

4. Have those users distinguished between smaller privately owned businesses and others in obtaining and processing financial information? For example, has such a distinction affected the degree of responsibility required of external accountants regarding financial statements (for example, audited, reviewed, or compiled)? If yes, how, what differences result, and why?
5. Have certain disclosures required by GAAP not been used by various users in making decisions about smaller privately owned businesses? If so, has the experience of those users differed in making decisions about large publicly owned businesses?
6.[14] Has the treatment of any items as required by GAAP not enhanced the benefits of the financial statements taken as a whole to various users in making decisions about smaller privately owned businesses? If yes, were adjustments made to reverse the treatment? Has the experience of those users differed in making decisions about large publicly owned businesses? Examples of items to consider are as follows:

---

[13]From FASB staff paper, June 26, 1981.

[14]Evidence about the benefits associated with the treatment of various items likely will be difficult to obtain. Nonetheless, because it is an aspect for which feedback would be helpful, it is listed here.

a. Capitalization of interest costs incurred on borrowed monies
b. Capitalization and subsequent amortization of leases and allocation of rental payments between principal and interest
c. Accounting for deferred income taxes.

7. What kinds of information required by GAAP may have enhanced the benefits of financial statements taken as a whole but have been difficult to understand, costly to provide and use, or both? What ways have been found to increase the understandability of that information or to reduce the cost? Was it simplified without significant loss of content?

8. Which users of financial statements of smaller privately owned businesses have virtually no access to financial information about a company other than from its financial statements?

9. What, if any, types of financial information not now required in GAAP financial statements do users who rely primarily on financial statements obtain, or at least desire, in making decisions about smaller privately owned businesses? In what circumstances is the information obtained, at what cost, and how used? Do those users obtain, or at least desire, the information in making decisions about large publicly owned businesses as well?

10. What factors have governed whether various smaller businesses provide GAAP financial statements or financial statements prepared on a different basis (for example, cash basis)? Who has decided? Have GAAP financial statements sometimes been provided for businesses for which financial statements prepared on some other basis would have been preferable and vice versa?

11. What factors have governed the degree of responsibility (audited, reviewed, or compiled) of the external accountant for the financial statements of various smaller businesses? In those instances in which compilation of financial statements was determined to be appropriate, what factors have governed whether the disclosures required by GAAP were provided? Who made these decisions?

12. How do the facts for areas 2-8, 10, and 11 differ for larger privately owned businesses than for smaller privately owned ones?

13. How do the facts for areas 2-8 and 10 differ for smaller publicly owned businesses than for smaller privately owned ones?

Appendix B

SURVEY QUESTIONNAIRES AND INSTRUCTIONS

REPORTING REQUIREMENTS OF PRIVATELY HELD COMPANIES

Sponsor: The Financial Accounting Standards Board. (FASB).

Supporting Organizations: National Association of Accountants
Robert Morris Associates
Various State Societies of CPAs

Objective: The primary objective of this project is to investigate reporting alternatives for privately held companies. This portion of the research is directed at identifying the factual basis needed for consideration of alternative structures for accounting principles.

Research Team: The project is carried out by a research team *independent* of the FASB. The team consists of A. R. Abdel-khalik, W. Collins, D. Shields, D. Snowball (all of the University of Florida), R. Stephens (The Ohio State University), and J. Wragge (the University of Delaware). (The team is assisted by an Advisory Committee which includes a manager of a privately held company.)

Correspondence: All correspondence is to be addressed to A. R. Abdel-khalik, Director, Accounting Research Center, University of Florida, Gainesville, Florida 32611.

Definitions:

1. Generally Accepted Accounting Principles (GAAP) consist of the accounting conventions, rules and procedures that are required by the accounting profession. For a CPA to report that a company's financial statements are prepared in accordance with GAAP, these rules and procedures must be followed.

2. Privately held companies are those companies that have no publicly traded stock.

Confidentiality: All responses will be kept absolutely confidential.

Results: Please enclose a business card or write your name and address below if you wish to receive a summary of the results.

Name: _____

Address: _____

_____

_____

_____

Telephone: _____

111

Question 1:

Please indicate which of the groups listed below are the users of the financial statements of your company, then rank them in terms of their importance to you.

(Please give the rank of one to the most important, and so on)

User groups	Check if applicable to your company	Rank of importance
Bank loan officers		
Bonding agencies		
Suppliers		
Owners not managing the company		
Management		
Others (please specify)		

112

In responding to some of the questions, the following *definitions* might be useful.

An Audit: is a comprehensive examination of the financial statement that permits an independent CPA to express an opinion that the statements are presented fairly in accordance with generally accepted accounting principles (or, if applicable, with another comprehensive basis of accounting).

A Review: is an engagement that, based on inquiry and analytical procedures, provides an independent CPA with a reasonable basis for expressing limited assurance that there are no material modifications that should be made to financial statements in order for them to be in conformity with generally accepted accounting principles or, if applicable, with another accounting basis.

A Compilation: is an engagement wherein a CPA presents in the form of financial statements information that is the representation of management (owners) without the CPA undertaking to express any assurance on the statements.

Question 2:

What services (if any) were provided for your company by CPA firms during the past year?

	Type of Service	Check as Applicable
1.	Audit of annual financial statements	_____
2.	Review of annual financial statements	_____
3.	Review of interim financial statements	_____
4.	Compilation of annual financial statements	_____
5.	Compilation of interim financial statements	_____
6.	Preparation of annual tax return	_____
7.	Other (please indicate)	

_____

_____

_____

_____

113

Question 3:

Owners of privately held companies have expressed varied opinions about accounting requirements in financial statements. Listed below is a number of specific accounting requirements in financial statements.

For each requirement, please check responses as applicable to your company.

Types of Accounting Requirements	The Accounting Requirement in Financial Statements is:						Is this accounting treatment followed in your company's annual financial statements?		
	Overly Complex		Relevant to manager's decision making		Relevant to outside users such as bankers				
	Yes	No	Yes	No	Yes	No	Yes	No	Not Applicable or Not Material
1. Capitalization of capital leases									
2. Capitalization of interest on construction									
3. Accounting for deferred taxes									
4. Preparing Statement of Changes in Financial Position									
5. Accounting for inventories at lower of cost or market									
6. Accounting for pensions prior to employee's retirement									
7. Discounting non-interest bearing long-term receivables and payables									
8. Accounting for contingencies									
9. Accounting for paid vacations when they are earned instead of when taken									

114

Question 4:

The following have been suggested as reasons for establishing a special set of generally accepted accounting principles for privately held companies (versus publicly held companies).

From your perspective, please indicate *the extent to which each is a valid reason.* Please check one response for each statement.

	Very Strong Reason	Strong Reason	Weak Reason	Very Weak Reason	Not Sure
1. It would increase the usefulness of financial statements to users outside the company					
2. It would reduce the degree of accounting sophistication demanded of small CPA firms					
3. It would reduce the cost to the CPA of keeping up with generally accepted accounting principles					
4. It would reduce the degree of accounting sophistication demanded of business managers					
5. It would enhance the usefulness of financial statements to management					
6. It would reduce the cost of applying generally accepted accounting principles					

7. Other (please specify)

_____

_____

_____

Question 5:

For how many years has your company employed the services of an independent CPA?

_____ years

Question 6:

To what extent do you agree that your CPA's continued involvement with your financial statements contributes to each of the following? (Please circle one answer for each item)

	Strongly Agree	Agree	Disagree	Strongly Disagree	Not Sure
1. Lower borrowing cost	4	3	2	1	0
2. Less restrictive loan covenants	4	3	2	1	0
3. More understandable data	4	3	2	1	0
4. Easier to finance through debt	4	3	2	1	0
5. More relevant data for managing your company	4	3	2	1	0
6. More reliable information for managing your company	4	3	2	1	0
7. Expected benefits for your company exceed the fees paid for a CPA's services	4	3	2	1	0
8. More relevant information for use by absentee owners	4	3	2	1	0

9. Other (please specify)

_____

_____

_____

Please comment on any of the above items about which you feel strongly.

_____

_____

_____

_____

Question 7:

In general, how important do you believe that each of the following factors is in obtaining bank loans (*not secured* by a specific collateral) for your company?

(Please circle one answer for each item)

	Very Important	Important	Unimportant	Very Unimportant	Not Sure
Type of Unsecured Loan:					
(a) Whether a long-term or short-term loan	4	3	2	1	0
(b) Whether or not obtained to finance a specific project	4	3	2	1	0
Size of Loan:					
(c) In terms of dollar amount	4	3	2	1	0
(d) In relationship to the total assets of your company	4	3	2	1	0
Company-related Information:					
(e) Knowing the banker	4	3	2	1	0
(f) Credit history	4	3	2	1	0
(g) Having your company's financial statements audited or reviewed	4	3	2	1	0
(h) Maintaining an accounting system for your use in decision making	4	3	2	1	0
(i) Adherence to generally accepted accounting principles even if an independent CPA was not involved	4	3	2	1	0
(j) Preparing quarterly financial statements for your company	4	3	2	1	0

(k) Please list any other factors that you think are important.

_____

_____

_____

Question 8:

A recent survey suggested a number of reasons for changes in the fees that CPAs charge their clients.

Please allocate 100 points to the following in terms of their importance as factors in determining the changes in the fees charged by CPAs during the past two years.

		Allocated Points
(a)	General inflationary conditions	_____
(b)	Better internal reporting to management	_____
(c)	Increase in accounting standards (complexity and number)	_____
(d)	Increase in business volume and transactions	_____
(e)	Others, please specify	_____
	Total number of points	___100___

Question 9:

(a) During the past fiscal year, the total fees your company paid to your CPA were approximately $ _____.

* * * * * *

(b) For the benefits provided by the CPA firm to your company, the fees charged were (please circle one):

Much too low	Too low	About right	Too high	Much too high

* * * * * *

(c) By what percentage would the fees charged by your CPA have to increase before you would consider the need to change the CPA firm?

Please circle a number:

10% or less   15%   20%   25%   30%   35%   40%   45%   50% or more

118

Our analysis of responses will be conducted in an aggregated form. No individual responses will be revealed. In order to assist us in properly classifying your response in the aggregate (group) profile, please complete the following information:

(A) *Concerning your company:*

    (a) Approximate total assets at most recent fiscal year end   _____

    (b) Approximate total sales for most recent fiscal year   _____

    (c) Number of full-time employees   _____

    (d) Number of owners (stockholders)   _____

    (e) Number of owners who are active in managing the company   _____

    (f) Are any of your company's securities registered with the Securities and Exchange Commission or other regulatory body? ( ) Yes ( ) No

    (g) Do you consider your company ( ) Small or ( ) Large?

(B) *Concerning your own involvement:*

    (a) Approximately how long have you been directly involved in preparing financial statements? _____ years

    (b) How important is each of the following in terms of its contribution to your knowledge of accounting: (Please check responses as applicable)

	Important	Unimportant	Not Applicable
(1) College			
(2) Formal training program			
(3) On the job experience			
(4) Professional reading (Wall Street Journal, etc.)			

What other information would you like to communicate to us?

_____
_____
_____
_____
_____
_____
_____
_____
_____
_____
_____
_____
_____
_____

Thank you for completing this questionnaire.

REPORTING REQUIREMENTS OF
PRIVATELY HELD COMPANIES

Sponsor: The Financial Accounting Standards Board.
(The FASB is the accounting body that sets accounting principles for financial reporting in the United States.)

Supporting Organizations: Robert Morris Associates.

Objective: The primary objective of this project is to gather facts concerning the use of financial statements of privately held companies.

Research Team: The project is carried out by a research team *independent* of the FASB. The team consists of A. R. Abdel-khalik, W. Collins, D. Shield, D. Snowball (all of the University of Florida), R. Stephens (The Ohio State University), and J. Wragge (the University of Delaware). (The team is assisted by an Advisory Committee which includes a banker.)

Correspondence: All correspondence is to be addressed to A. R. Abdel khalik, Director, Accounting Research Center, University of Florida, Gainesville, Florida 32611.

Definitions:
1. Generally Accepted Accounting Principles (GAAP) consist of the accounting conventions, rules and procedures that are required by the accounting profession. For a CPA to report that a company's financial statements are prepared in accordance with GAAP, these rules and procedures must be followed.

2. Privately held companies are those companies that have no publicly traded stock.

Confidentiality: All responses will be kept absolutely confidential.

Results: Please write your name and address below (or enclose a business card) if you wish to receive a summary of the results.

Name: _____

Address: _____

_____

_____

_____

Telephone: _____

The following flow chart is a simplified description of certain lending decisions. The objective of this flow chart is to assist in focusing on the issues of relevance to this study.

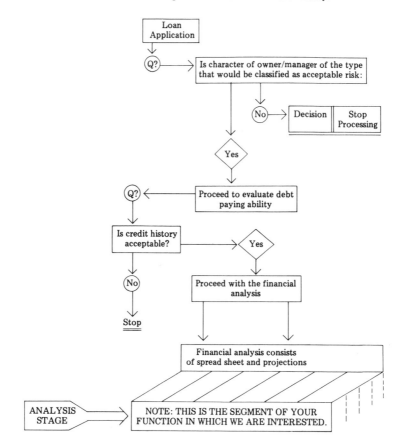

ALL THE QUESTIONS THAT FOLLOW
PERTAIN TO THE *ANALYSIS STAGE*
INDICATED BY THE ABOVE FLOW CHART

Question 1:

Approximately how many loan applications made by privately held companies have you processed (in the Analysis Stage) during the past two years?

Number _____

Question 2:

Consider the loan applications made by privately held companies in the last two years that reached the Analysis Stage and that contained financial statements that:

(a) were prepared in accordance with generally accepted accounting principles,
and (b) were *audited, reviewed,* or *compiled* by an independent CPA.

In general, what has been your evaluation of the financial statements having these characteristics that you processed during the past two years: (please circle a number for *each* dimension)

	Very High	High	Average	Low	Very Low
(1) Degree of usefulness of the financial statements for projecting *amounts* of cash flows					
(a) if audited	5	4	3	2	1
(b) if reviewed	5	4	3	2	1
(c) if compiled	5	4	3	2	1
(2) Degree of usefulness of the financial statements for projecting the *timing* of cash flows					
(a) if audited	5	4	3	2	1
(b) if reviewed	5	4	3	2	1
(c) if compiled	5	4	3	2	1
(3) Degree of your *confidence* in projections of cash flows based on the financial statements					
(a) if audited	5	4	3	2	1
(b) if reviewed	5	4	3	2	1
(c) if compiled	5	4	3	2	1
(4) Degree of *reliability* of information presented in the financial statements					
(a) if audited	5	4	3	2	1
(b) if reviewed	5	4	3	2	1
(c) if compiled	5	4	3	2	1

Question 3:

A number of cases reflecting various financial reporting characteristics of loan applications that may have reached the Analysis Stage are listed below. Please consider each of these characteristics separately.

* * * * * * * *

CASE A: NONCANCELLABLE FINANCING OR CAPITAL LEASES WERE NOT CAPITALIZED.

1. How frequently have you encountered this characteristic during the past two years? (please circle a response)

Highly frequently   7   6   5   4   3   2   1   Highly infrequently

2. When you encountered this characteristic, what additional information (if any) did you typically request?

3. When you encountered the characteristic stated above and requested information, how frequently were you successful in obtaining that information? (please circle a response)

Highly frequently   5   4   3   2   1   Highly infrequently

4. In what ways (if any) have you typically adjusted the data to fit your information needs for making financial analysis?

5. When you encountered this characteristic, what other actions did you typically take? (please check as appropriate)

    a. made the loans with more restrictive covenants   _____
    b. made the loans at higher interest rates   _____
    c. reduced the size of the loan   _____
    d. none   _____
    e. other, please specify   _____

Continue Question 3:

CASE B: INTEREST ON CONSTRUCTION WAS NOT CAPITALIZED.

1. How frequently have you encountered this characteristic during the past two years? (please circle a response)

Highly frequently   7   6   5   4   3   2   1   Highly infrequently

2. When you encountered this characteristic, what additional information (if any) did you typically request?

_____

_____

_____

_____

3. When you encountered the characteristic stated above and requested information, how frequently were you successful in obtaining that information? (please circle a response)

Highly frequently   5   4   3   2   1   Highly infrequently

4. In what ways (if any) have you typically adjusted the data to fit your information needs for making financial analysis?

_____

_____

_____

_____

5. When you encountered this characteristic, what other actions did you typically take? (please check as appropriate)

     a. made the loans with more restrictive covenants   _____
     b. made the loans at higher interest rates   _____
     c. reduced the size of the loan   _____
     d. other, please specify

_____

_____

_____

_____

* * * * * * * *

Continue Question 3:

CASE C: DEFERRED TAXES WERE NOT ACCOUNTED FOR.

1. How frequently have you encountered this characteristic during the past two years? (please circle a response)

Highly frequently   7   6   5   4   3   2   1   Highly infrequently

2. When you encountered this characteristic, what additional information (if any) did you typically request?

_____

_____

_____

_____

3. When you encountered the characteristic stated above and requested information, how frequently were you successful in obtaining that information? (please circle a response)

Highly frequently   5   4   3   2   1   Highly infrequently

4. In what ways (if any) have you typically adjusted the data to fit your information needs for making financial analysis?

_____

_____

_____

_____

5. When you encountered this characteristic, what other actions did you typically take? (please check as appropriate)

    a. made the loans with more restrictive covenants   _____
    b. made the loans at higher interest rates   _____
    c. reduced the size of the loan   _____
    d. other, please specify   _____

_____

_____

_____

* * * * * * * * *

Continue Question 3:

CASE D: STATEMENT OF CHANGES IN THE FINANCIAL POSITION WAS NOT PREPARED.

1. How frequently have you encountered this characteristic during the past two years? (please circle a response)

Highly frequently   7   6   5   4   3   2   1   Highly infrequently

2. When you encountered this characteristic, what additional information (if any) did you typically request?

_____

_____

_____

_____

3. When you encountered the characteristic stated above and requested information, how frequently were you successful in obtaining that information? (please circle a response)

Highly frequently   5   4   3   2   1   Highly infrequently

4. In what ways (if any) have you typically adjusted the data to fit your information needs for making financial analysis?

_____

_____

_____

_____

5. When you encountered this characteristic, what other actions did you typically take? (please check as appropriate)

a. made the loans with more restrictive covenants   _____
b. made the loans at higher interest rates   _____
c. reduced the size of the loan   _____
d. other, please specify   _____

_____

_____

_____

_____

* * * * * * * *

Question 4:

The following have been suggested by some individuals as reasons why bank loan officers might prefer financial statements that are prepared in accordance with generally accepted accounting principles as compared to other accounting bases.

From your perspective, please indicate the extent to which each is a valid reason.

Reasons	Very Strong	Strong	Weak	Very Weak	Not Sure
1. Because they provide more relevant information	4	3	2	1	0
2. Because they enable a better evaluation of debt paying ability	4	3	2	1	0
3. Because the bank policy requires that information	4	3	2	1	0
4. Because it represents evidence of the loan officer's diligence	4	3	2	1	0
5. Because they indicate a higher level of CPA involvement	4	3	2	1	0
6. Because they provide more reliable information	4	3	2	1	0
7. Because they are a deterrent to high risk clients	4	3	2	1	0
8. Because they permit comparability between companies	4	3	2	1	0

9. Others (please specify)

_____

_____

_____

_____

Question 5:

Please indicate the extent to which you have found the items listed below useful in analyzing the financial statements of privately held companies:

(Please circle one answer for *each* item)

Information Item	Very Useful	Useful	Occasion-ally Useful	Useless	Not Sure
1. Aging of receivables	4	3	2	1	0
2. Market values of inventories	4	3	2	1	0
3. Client's projections of cash flows	4	3	2	1	0
4. Data on construction in progress	4	3	2	1	0
5. Appraised values of buildings and equipment	4	3	2	1	0
6. The cost of replacing fixed assets	4	3	2	1	0

7. Others (please specify)

_____

_____

_____

_____

129

Question 6:

For each of the following, please indicate whether the items listed below should be required to be included in the footnotes to the financial statements.

Item	Should the item be required to be reported in the footnotes to the financial statements?	
1. Aging of receivables	( ) yes	( ) no
2. Market values of inventories	( ) yes	( ) no
3. Client's projections of cash flows	( ) yes	( ) no
4. Data on contracts in progress	( ) yes	( ) no
5. Appraised values of buildings and equipment	( ) yes	( ) no
6. The cost of replacing fixed assets	( ) yes	( ) no

7. Others, please indicate

_____

_____

_____

_____

Question 7: (Concerning the *Accounting Basis*)

The following characteristics are claimed to be associated with financial statements of *privately held companies that are prepared in accordance with generally accepted accounting principles* as compared to other bases such as the cash basis. To what extent do you agree?

Please comment on any of these characteristics below.

	Strongly Agree	Agree	Disagree	Strongly Disagree	Not Sure
1. Lower borrowing cost	4	3	2	1	0
2. Less restrictive loan covenants	4	3	2	1	0
3. More understandable data	4	3	2	1	0
4. Excessive accounting fees for the independent CPAs	4	3	2	1	0
5. Easier to finance through debt	4	3	2	1	0
6. More relevant data for managing the company	4	3	2	1	0
7. More reliable information for managing the company	4	3	2	1	0
8. Expected benefits to the company exceed the cost of preparing financial statements	4	3	2	1	0
9. More relevant information for use by absentee owners	4	3	2	1	0
10. More reliable information for use by the loan officers	4	3	2	1	0

11. Other (please specify)

_____

_____

Comments: _____

_____

_____

_____

131

Question 8:

Please indicate the extent to which you agree that each of the following accounting treatments should continue to be required for reporting by *small* privately held companies.

(Please circle one number for each item)

	Strongly Agree	Agree	Disagree	Strongly Disagree	Not Sure
1. Capitalizing of interest on construction	4	3	2	1	0
2. Capitalizing of capital leases	4	3	2	1	0
3. Accounting for deferred taxes	4	3	2	1	0
4. Accounting for investment in other company stocks on the equity basis	4	3	2	1	0
5. Preparing Statement of Changes in Financial Position	4	3	2	1	0
6. Accounting for inventories at lower of cost or market	4	3	2	1	0
7. Accounting for pensions prior to employees' retirement	4	3	2	1	0
8. Reporting long term payables and receivables at present values	4	3	2	1	0
9. Accounting for paid vacations when they are earned instead of when taken	4	3	2	1	0
10. Accounting for contingencies	4	3	2	1	0

Please state reasons for your responses below.

_____

_____

_____

_____

_____

Question 9:

Please indicate your agreement or disagreement with each of the following propositions:

(Please circle a response for each item)

	Strongly Agree	Agree	Disagree	Strongly Disagree	Not Sure
1. Although most privately held companies have fewer or simpler activities than do most publicly held companies, they cannot account for those activities differently without making the financial statements less useful to you.	4	3	2	1	0
2. When you make decisions about privately held companies, you typically need the same information as when you make decisions about publicly held companies.	4	3	2	1	0
3. When you make decisions about privately held companies, you generally rely less on financial statements of those companies than when you make decisions about publicly held companies.	4	3	2	1	0
4. You generally are able to obtain more information (beyond that reported in financial statements) from privately held client companies than from publicly held client companies.	4	3	2	1	0
5. Your privately held client companies show more concern about the cost of providing financial statements than do your publicly held client companies.	4	3	2	1	0

Question 10:

Consider loan applications made to your bank by (1) small privately held companies and (2) large privately held companies.

(a) Do the same lending officers typically evaluate loan applications from each type of company?

(   ) yes   (   ) no

(b) Do lending officers typically expect the same level of disclosure in the financial statements of each type of company?

(   ) yes   (   ) no

(c) If your response to item (b) above is "no," please indicate the specific areas where you would expect differences.

_____

_____

_____

_____

(d) Do lending officers expect the same accounting principles to be followed by each type of company?

(   ) yes   (   ) no

(e) If you checked "no" above, please indicate the specific accounting principles where differences occur.

_____

_____

_____

_____

Question 11:

If you answered "no" to any of the inquiries made in Question 10, please indicate the level of each of the factors listed below that you typically use in classifying privately held companies as either small or large.

(a) Total sales in dollars $_____

(b) Total assets in dollars $_____

(c) Number of employees   _____

(d) Number of persons employed by the
    client company as internal accountants _____

(e) Other, please specify:

_____

_____

_____

_____

Question 12:

Please provide us with the following information about your bank:

1. Number of branches   _____

2. Number of Senior Vice Presidents   _____

3. Total assets   _____

4. Total demand deposits   _____

5. Total time deposits   _____

Thank you for completing this questionnaire. Since analysis of responses will be conducted in an aggregated form, we also would like to generate an aggregated profile of the respondents. The information requested below is optional. However, we would appreciate your completing it.

Question 13:

(a) Approximately how long have you been:

(i) a bank lender _____ years
(ii) directly involved in using
financial statements _____ years

(b) How important was each of the following sources in terms of its contribution to your knowledge of accounting:

	Important	Unimportant	Not Applicable
(1) College accounting courses			
(2) Other formal training programs			
(3) On the job experience			
(4) Professional reading (Wall Street Journal, etc.)			

Question 14:

What other information would you like to communicate to us?

_____

_____

_____

_____

_____

_____

_____

_____

Thank you for completing this questionnaire.

REPORTING REQUIREMENTS OF
PRIVATELY HELD COMPANIES

Sponsor: The Financial Accounting Standards Board. (FASB).

Supporting Organizations: National Association of Accountants
Robert Morris Associates
Various State Societies of CPAs

Objective: The primary objective of this project is to investigate reporting alternatives for privately held companies. This portion of the research is directed at identifying the factual basis needed for consideration of alternative structures for accounting principles.

Research Team: The project is to be completed by a research team independent of the FASB. The team consists of A. R. Abdel-khalik, W. Collins, D. Shields, D. Snowball (all of the University of Florida), R. Stephens (The Ohio State University), and J. Wragge (the University of Delaware). The research team is assisted by an advisory committee that includes a practitioner.

Correspondence: All correspondence is to be addressed to A. R. Abdel-khalik, Director, Accounting Research Center, University of Florida, Gainesville, Florida 32611.

Definitions:
1. Generally Accepted Accounting Principles (GAAP) consist of the accounting conventions, rules and procedures that are required by the accounting profession. For a CPA to report that a company's financial statements are prepared in accordance with GAAP, these rules and procedures must be followed.

2. Privately held companies are those companies that have no publicly traded stock.

Confidentiality: All responses will be kept absolutely confidential.

Results: Please enclose a business card or write your name and address below if you wish to receive a summary of the results.

Name: _____

Address: _____

_____

_____

_____

Telephone: _____

Question 1:

Please rank the following in terms of the importance that you believe they attach to the financial statements of privately held companies (the group attaching the most importance to financial statements should be ranked 1 and so on).

Group	Rank
Bank loan officers	
Bonding agencies	
Suppliers	
Owners who are not managing the company	
Management	
Others (please specify)	

Question 2:

Listed below are several accounting treatments required by Generally Accepted Accounting Principles. For each treatment, please complete the following information concerning the financial statements of privately held companies.

Types of Accounting Treatment	The Accounting Treatment is:					
	Overly Complex		Relevant to Managers' Decision Making		Relevant to Outside Users Such as Bankers	
	Yes	No	Yes	No	Yes	No
1. Capitalizing capital leases						
2. Capitalizing interest on construction						
3. Accounting for deferred taxes						
4. Preparing Statement of Changes in Financial Position						
5. Accounting for inventories at lower of cost or market						
6. Accounting for pensions						
7. Discounting long-term non-interest bearing receivables and payables						
8. Accounting for contingencies						
9. Accounting for paid vacations when they are earned instead of when taken						
10. Accounting for investments in other company stocks on the equity basis						

Question 3:

Consider situations in the last two years in which you have assisted managers of privately held companies in preparing annual financial statements.

For each of the accounting areas listed below (where dollar amounts were material) please indicate the approximate percentage of cases for which the selection was made:

    (a) *to follow GAAP,*
or   (b) *not to follow GAAP.*

Please consider each area and each company size separately.

Accounting Areas	Relative Company Size	Approximate percentage of the time you	
		elected to follow GAAP	elected not to follow GAAP
1. Capitalizing	Small	%	%
capital leases	Large	%	%
2. Capitalizing interest	Small	%	%
on construction	Large	%	%
3. Accounting for	Small	%	%
deferred taxes	Large	%	%
4. Inventory	Small	%	%
valuation	Large	%	%
5. Accounting	Small	%	%
for pensions	Large	%	%
6. Investment in related	Small	%	%
companies	Large	%	%
7. Accounting for	Small	%	%
contingencies	Large	%	%
8. Compensated	Small	%	%
absences	Large	%	%
9. Statement of Changes	Small	%	%
in the Financial Position	Large	%	%
10. Discounting long-term	Small	%	%
receivables and payables	Large	%	%

Question 4:

Consider those cases in the previous question where the decision was made not to follow GAAP. For each of the following accounting areas, please rank the reasons listed below in terms of their importance in the decision not to follow GAAP. For each accounting area, rank the most important as 1, and so forth)

Accounting Area	The non-GAAP treatment was adopted because the item was:		
	more relevant to owners	less costly	consistent with the particular accounting basis used
1. Capitalization of capital leases			
2. Capitalization of interest on construction			
3. Accounting for deferred taxes			
4. Inventory valuation			
5. Accounting for pensions			
6. Investment in related companies			
7. Accounting for contingencies			
8. Compensated absences			
9. Statement of Changes in Financial Position			
10. Discounting long-term receivables and payables			

Question 5:

The following have been suggested as reasons for establishing a special set of generally accepted accounting principles for privately held companies versus publicly held companies.

From your perspective, please indicate the extent to which each is a valid reason. For each statement please circle one number for relatively *small* and one number for relatively *large* privately held companies.

	Relative Company Size	Very Strong Reason	Strong Reason	Weak Reason	Very Weak Reason	Not Sure
1. Would increase the usefulness of financial statements to users outside the company	Small	4	3	2	1	0
	Large	4	3	2	1	0
2. Would reduce the degree of accounting sophistication demanded of small CPA firms	Small	4	3	2	1	0
	Large	4	3	2	1	0
3. Would reduce the cost to the CPA of keeping up with Generally Accepted Accounting Principles	Small	4	3	2	1	0
	Large	4	3	2	1	0
4. Would reduce the degree of accounting sophistication demanded of business managers	Small	4	3	2	1	0
	Large	4	3	2	1	0
5. Would enhance the usefulness of financial statements to management	Small	4	3	2	1	0
	Large	4	3	2	1	0
6. Would reduce the cost of applying Generally Accepted Accounting Principles	Small	4	3	2	1	0
	Large	4	3	2	1	0

7. Other (please specify)

_____

_____

_____

142

Question 6:

Please indicate the extent to which you agree that each of the following accounting treatments should continue to be required by GAAP for reporting by privately held companies.

(Please circle one number for each item)

	Strongly Agree	Agree	Disagree	Strongly Disagree	Not Sure
1. Capitalizing interest on construction	4	3	2	1	0
2. Capitalizing capital leases	4	3	2	1	0
3. Accounting for deferred taxes	4	3	2	1	0
4. Accounting for investment in other company stocks on the equity basis	4	3	2	1	0
5. Preparing Statement of Changes in Financial Position	4	3	2	1	0
6. Accounting for inventories at lower of cost or market	4	3	2	1	0
7. Reporting long-term payables and receivables at present values	4	3	2	1	0
8. Accounting for paid vacations when they are earned instead of when taken	4	3	2	1	0
9. Accounting for contingencies	4	3	2	1	0
10. Accounting for pensions	4	3	2	1	0

Please elaborate on your responses below.

_____

_____

_____

_____

143

Question 7:

Referring to your answers in the previous question (Question 6) in what ways and for which items would your answers differ for publicly held companies?

_____

_____

_____

_____

_____

Question 8:

Consider the situations in which financial statements:

(a) are prepared in accordance with generally accepted accounting principles, and

(b) are prepared with various types of involvement of an independent CPA (audit, review, or compilation).

In general, what would be your evaluation of the financial statements of privately held companies in each of the situations listed below?

	CPA Involvement	Very High	High	Average	Low	Very Low
1. Degree of usefulness of these financial statements for projecting *amounts* of cash flows	(1) Audit	4	3	2	1	0
	(2) Review	4	3	2	1	0
	(3) Compilation	4	3	2	1	0
2. Degree of usefulness of of these financial statements for projecting the *timing* of cash flows	(1) Audit	4	3	2	1	0
	(2) Review	4	3	2	1	0
	(3) Compilation	4	3	2	1	0
3. Degree of your confidence in projection of cash flows based on these financial statements	(1) Audit	4	3	2	1	0
	(2) Review	4	3	2	1	0
	(3) Compilation	4	3	2	1	0
4. Degree of reliability of the information presented in these financial statements	(1) Audit	4	3	2	1	0
	(2) Review	4	3	2	1	0
	(3) Compilation	4	3	2	1	0

Question 9:

Please indicate your agreement or disagreement with each of the following propositions:

(Please circle one answer for each item)

	Strongly Agree	Agree	Disagree	Strongly Disagree	Not Sure
1. Although most privately held companies have fewer or simpler activities than do most publicly held companies, they cannot account for those activities differently without reducing the usefulness of financial information to those who make decisions about them.	4	3	2	1	0
2. Those who make decisions about privately held companies have essentially the same information needs as those who make decisions about publicly held companies.	4	3	2	1	0
3. Those who make decisions about privately held companies generally rely less on financial statements of the companies than do those who make decisions about publicly held companies.	4	3	2	1	0
4. Those who make decisions about privately held companies generally have more ability to obtain information beyond that reported in the financial statements from those companies than do those who make decisions about publicly held companies.	4	3	2	1	0
5. The costs of providing financial statements are relatively greater for a privately held company than for publicly held companies.	4	3	2	1	0

Question 10:

Under what circumstances, if any, would preparing annual financial statements of privately held companies on a tax-basis be acceptable?

Please check as applicable:

a. When the financial statements are intended for use by owners only _____

b. When the financial statements are intended for use by bank loan officers for secured loans _____

c. When the financial statements are intended for use by suppliers _____

d. Other circumstances (please specify):

_____

_____

_____

_____

_____

_____

Question 11:

Consider the choice between financial statements prepared in accordance with GAAP as compared to other bases (such as tax or cash basis).

In your opinion, why might bank loan officers and other lenders prefer financial statements that *are prepared in accordance with generally accepted accounting principles?*

(Please circle one number for each statement)

	Very Strong Reason	Strong Reason	Weak Reason	Very Weak Reason	Not Sure
1. Because they provide more relevant information	4	3	2	1	0
2. Because they enable a better evaluation of debt paying ability	4	3	2	1	0
3. Because the bank requires that information	4	3	2	1	0
4. Because it represents evidence of diligence by the loan officer	4	3	2	1	0
5. Because they indicate a higher level of CPA involvement	4	3	2	1	0
6. Because they are a deterrent to high risk clients	4	3	2	1	0
7. Because they permit comparability between companies	4	3	2	1	0

8. Others (please specify)

_____

_____

_____

_____

Question 12:

A recent survey suggested a number of reasons for changes in the fees charged by CPAs .

Please allocate 100 points to the following in terms of their importance as factors in determining the changes in the fees charged by CPAs during the past two years.

		Allocated points
(a)	General inflationary conditions	_____
(b)	Improve reporting for management uses	_____
(c)	Increase in accounting standards (complexity and number)	_____
(d)	Increase in business volume and transactions	_____
(e)	Others, please specify	_____
	Total number of points	100

_____

_____

_____

_____

_____

Question 13:

(a)   At the current rate of promulgating financial accounting standards, how many *hours per year* do you think a practicing CPA must devote to remain current with GAAP?

Answer: _____ hours per year.

(b)   How many hours per year do you believe that a practitioner in a firm of the same size as yours spends in trying to keep current with GAAP?

Answer: _____ hours per year.

(c)   If the number you wrote in reponding to item (a) is higher than that you wrote in responding to item (b) above, how do you believe the gap should be closed?

Please check as applicable:

____ Reduce the rate at which accounting standards are promulgated.

____ Permit other accounting bases for privately held companies (such as the tax basis) without opinion qualification.

____ Train users of financial statements of privately held companies to accept disclaimers and qualified opinions for specific deviations from GAAP.

____ Allow individual practitioners to deviate from certain GAAP standards for privately held companies without qualifying the audit opinion.

Other: please specify _____

_____

_____

_____

_____

Question 14:

The following characteristics are claimed to be associated with financial statements of *privately held companies* that are prepared *in accordance with generally accepted accounting principles* as compared to other bases such as the cash basis. To what extent do you agree?

	Strongly Agree	Agree	Disagree	Strongly Disagree	Not Sure
1. Lower borrowing cost	4	3	2	1	0
2. Less restrictive loan covenants	4	3	2	1	0
3. More understandable data	4	3	2	1	0
4. Excessive accounting fees for the independent CPAs	4	3	2	1	0
5. Easier to finance through debt	4	3	2	1	0
6. More relevant data for managing the company	4	3	2	1	0
7. More reliable information for managing the company	4	3	2	1	0
8. Expected benefits to the company exceed the cost of preparing financial statements	4	3	2	1	0
9. More relevant information for use by absentee owners	4	3	2	1	0
10. More reliable information for use by loan officers	4	3	2	1	0

11. Other (please specify)

_____

_____

If you would like to comment on your responses to any of the above items, please do so below:

_____

_____

_____

_____

150

Question 15:

Consider the financial statements (prepared with the involvement of a CPA) of (1) small privately held companies, and (2) large privately held companies.

(a) Is the same level of disclosure generally provided in the financial statements of each type of company?

( ) Yes   ( ) No

(b) If your response to item (a) above is "no", please indicate the specific areas where you would expect differences.

(c) Are the same accounting principles generally followed in the financial statements of each type of company?

( ) Yes   ( ) No

(d) If you checked "no" above, please indicate the specific accounting principles where differences occur.

Question 16:

If you answered "no" to any of the inquiries made in the previous question (Question 15), please indicate the level of each of the factors listed below that you typically use in classifying privately held companies as either small or large.

(a) Total sales in dollars $ _____
(b) Total assets in dollars $ _____
(c) Number of employees   _____
(d) Number of persons employed by the client
    as internal accountants   _____
(e) Other, please specify:

_____

_____

_____

_____

_____

Question 17:

For each item, please check the column that best describes *your accounting firm:*

Item	$0-5$	$6-10$	$11-20$	$21-40$	Over 40
Number of partners or equivalent					
Number of clients that are private companies (rather than public companies)					
Number of clients that are public companies					

Question 18:

(a) How long have you been a practicing CPA?

_____ years

(b) What other information would you like to communicate to the researchers?

_____

_____

_____

_____

_____

_____

_____

_____

_____

Thank you for completing this questionnaire.

REFERENCES

Alderman, C. Wayne; Guy, Dan M.; and Meals, Dennis R. "Other Comprehensive Bases of Accounting: Alternatives to GAAP?" *Journal of Accountancy,* August 1982, pp. 52-62.

American Institute of Accountants, Report of Study Group on Business Income. *Changing Concepts of Business Income.* New York: Macmillan Company, 1952.

American Institute of Certified Public Accountants. Statement on Auditing Standards No. 14, *Special Reports.* New York: AICPA, 1977.

_____. "The 'GAAP II' Movement: Now or Never?" *PCPS Reporter,* October 1980, p. 2.

_____, Accounting and Review Services Committee. Statement No. 1, *Compilation and Review of Financial Statements.* New York: AICPA, December 1978.

_____, Accounting Standards Division, Committee on Generally Accepted Accounting Principles for Smaller and/or Closely Held Businesses. *Report of the Committee on Generally Accepted Accounting Principles for Smaller and/or Closely Held Businesses.* New York: AICPA, August 1976.

_____, Private Companies Practice Section, Technical Issues Committee. *Sunset Review of Accounting Principles.* New York: AICPA, 1982.

_____, Special Committee on Accounting Standards Overload. *Tentative Conclusions and Recommendations of the Special Committee on Accounting Standards Overload.* New York: AICPA, December 1981.

_____, Special Committee on Small and Medium Sized Firms. *Report of the Special Committee on Small and Medium Sized Firms.* New York: AICPA, October 1980.

Armstrong, Marshall S. "The Impact of FASB Statements on Small Business." *Journal of Accountancy,* August 1977, pp. 88-90.

Arnstein, Peter. "Arnstein Opinion." *The Journal of Accountancy,* December 1972, pp. 83 and 84.

Benis, Martin. "Rational Small Business Exceptions to FASB Rules." *The CPA Journal,* February 1978, pp. 33-37.

Benjamin, James J., and Stanga, Keith G. "Differences in Disclosure Needs of Major Users of Financial Statements." *Accounting and Business Research,* Summer 1977, pp. 187-192.

Block, Max. "Duality in the Accounting Profession." *The CPA Journal,* July 1974, pp. 29-34.

————. "Trend to Duality in Accounting Standards." *The CPA Journal,* March 1977, pp. 11-15.

Campbell, Jane E. "'Big GAAP—Little GAAP': The Effect on Bank Loan Officers." Working paper. Ohio: College of Administrative Science, Ohio State University, September 1982.

Chazen, Charles, and Benson, Benjamin. "Fitting GAAP to Smaller Businesses." *Journal of Accountancy,* February 1978, pp. 46-51.

Falk, Haim; Gobdel, Bruce G.; and Naus, James H. "Disclosure for Closely Held Corporations." *Journal of Accountancy,* October 1976, pp. 85-89.

Financial Accounting Standards Advisory Council, Task Force on GAAP Requirements of Concern to Small or Closely Held Businesses. *Report of Task Force on GAAP Requirements of Concern to Small or Closely Held Businesses.* FASAC, December 1978.

FASB Concepts Statement No. 2, *Qualitative Characteristics of Accounting Information.* Stamford, Conn.: FASB, May 1980.

FASB Invitation to Comment, *Financial Reporting by Private and Small Public Companies.* Stamford, Conn.: FASB, November 20, 1981.

FASB Invitation to Comment, *Financial Statements and Other Means of Financial Reporting.* Stamford, Conn.: FASB, May 12, 1980.

FASB Statement No. 13, *Accounting for Leases.* Stamford, Conn.: FASB, November 1976.

FASB Statement No. 21, *Suspension of the Reporting of Earnings per Share and Segment Information by Nonpublic Enterprises.* Stamford, Conn.: FASB, April 1978.

FASB Statement No. 33, *Financial Reporting and Changing Prices.* Stamford, Conn.: FASB, September 1979.

FASB Statement No. 35, *Accounting and Reporting by Defined Benefit Pension Plans.* Stamford, Conn.: FASB, March 1980.

FASB Statement No. 36, *Disclosure of Pension Information.* Stamford, Conn.: FASB, May 1980.

FASB Statement No. 69, *Disclosures about Oil and Gas Producing Activities.* Stamford, Conn.: FASB, November 1982.

Hepp, Gerald W., and McRae, Thomas W. "Accounting Standards Overload: Relief Is Needed." *Journal of Accountancy,* May 1982, pp. 52-62.